The Catholic Prayer Book

The Catholic Prayer Book

Compiled by
Msgr. Michael Buckley

Edited by
Tony Castle

SERVANT BOOKS
Ann Arbor, Michigan

First American Edition 1986
by Servant Books
   P.O. Box 8617
   Ann Arbor, Michigan 48107

First published in 1984 in
Great Britain by Hodder and
Stoughton

Concordat cum originali: John P. Dewis
Imprimatur: Rt. Rev. Thomas McMahon
   Bishop of Brentwood
30 April, 1984

Paperback edition
ISBN 0-89283-283-5

Leather bound edition
ISBN 0-89283-314-9

Contents

Introduction   xiii
How to use the Prayer Book   xvii

The Christian Vocation   1

Prayers to God the Father   3
   Thanksgiving and praise for Creation, Faith
      and Salvation, including psalms 136, 8, 112,
      66, 137, 29, 144.
   Magnificat   16

Prayers to God the Son   19
   Jesus Psalter   19
   The Litany of the Sacred Heart   30
   The Way of the Cross   33
   Devotion to the Five Sacred Wounds   40

Prayers to the Holy Spirit   44
   For the presence of the Holy Spirit   44
      including Come Holy Spirit   44
   For the Gifts of the Holy Spirit   48

The Sacraments   51

Baptism   55
   Renewal of Baptismal Vows   55
   Prayers for parents, godparents and all baptised   56

Eucharist:
   Sacrament and Sacrifice   59

The Sacrifice: the Mass   61
   Prayers before Mass, including
   psalms 121, 99, 83   61

The order of Mass   67
Eucharistic Prayer I   76
Eucharistic Prayer II   80
Eucharistic Prayer III   83
Eucharistic Prayer IV   87
Prayers after Mass   94

The Sacrament   96

Prayers before Holy Communion   96
Prayers after Holy Communion   102
   including Prayer before a crucifix   103
Anima Christi   103
Prayers before the Blessed Sacrament   105
   including Adoro te devote   106
Eucharistic Exposition and Benediction   115

Reconciliation   121

Prayers before the Sacrament of Reconciliation
   including psalms 6, 31, 37, 50, 101, 129, 142   122
Prayers after the Sacrament of Reconciliation
   including psalm 102   127

Prayer

Daily Prayers   135
   General Prayers   135
   The Lord's Prayer   135
   The Hail Mary   135
   The Apostles' Creed   136
   The Confiteor   136
   Acts of Faith, Hope and Charity   137
   Short Acts   138
   At the day's beginning   139
   To the Holy Trinity   139
   To God the Father   140
   To God the Son   149
      including The Prayer of Saint Francis   150
   Saint Patrick's Breastplate   152
   At the day's close   155
   To the Holy Trinity   155
   To God the Father   156
   To God the Son   159
   To the Holy Spirit   160

Blessings	161
Nunc dimittis	163
General night prayers	163

Family Prayer — 166

For the family: parents and children	166
Grace before meals	170
Grace after meals	170
A Selection of Graces	170

Praying Continually — 173

The Jesus Prayer	173
Litany of the Holy Name	173
Aspirations or short prayers	177

Special Occasions — 182

Prayers from the Roman Missal	182
Prayers from other sources	194
including For the Church	194
For the Pope	195
For Vocations	195
For Remembrance Sunday	198
For Peace	199
Prayers for spiritual growth	206
including Love of God	209
Prayers in times of sickness and healing	223
A blessing for the sick	232
Prayers for the dying	233

Mary, Mother of the Church — 235

Prayers to Our Lady	235
Hail Holy Queen	235
Memorare	236
The Angelus	236
The Regina Coeli	237
Thirty Days Prayer	241
The Rosary	245
The Joyful Mysteries	245
The Sorrowful Mysteries	247
The Glorious Mysteries	248
Litany of Our Lady	249

The Angels and Saints — 252

Prayers to the Saints	252

Saint Joseph   253
Saints Peter and Paul   254
Patron Saints   255
Litany of the Saints   259

Holy Souls   264
Prayers for the dead   264
Bona Mors   267

Acknowledgements   271

The Catholic Prayer Book represents a fine attempt to re-establish a venerable Catholic tradition, namely the personal prayerbook. The editor, Monsignor Michael Buckley, has culled excellent prayers from the Catholic treasury of the past and present, with a very serious attempt at producing an updated prayer book replete with quotations from the saints and from spiritual writers of the present, as well as from great sources of other world religions. He has provided us with a valuable companion for every Catholic interested in personal prayer.

By including basic liturgical prayers and sacramental prayers along with inspirational meditations, *The Catholic Prayer Book* restores a sense of balance in the devotional life of clergy, religious and laity. The book is clearly compiled with a sense of that unique devotion which has characterized Catholic piety throughout the ages and yet it is thoroughly contemporary. I highly endorse *The Catholic Prayer Book*.

—Cardinal John O'Connor
Archbishop of New York

The Holy Spirit is the inspirer of all prayer. All through the centuries the prayer life of Christians has been lived under the influence of the Holy Spirit. Many of the well-known prayers of the Saints, hallowed by use and set down in print, have been of inestimable value in the spiritual lives of countless millions of Christians. The Spirit, too, is alive in our times and many contemporary prayers speak to the soul of modern man. This is all the work of the Holy Spirit.

Many ancient prayers are relevant to today's age precisely because they were inspired by the Holy Spirit. *The Catholic Prayer Book* gathers the old and the new prayers as part of our Christian heritage. Monsignor Michael Buckley 'is like a householder who brings out from his storeroom things both new and old' (Matthew 13:52). The prayers in the prayer book belong to the Church. I hope its use will bring all Christians closer together, but above all closer to God, because the power of prayer is the Spirit at work in our lives and world.

Cardinal Basil Hume
Archbishop of Westminster

Introduction

*P*rayer is as natural to us as breathing. For Christians both are necessary for life. The way in which we Christians pray reflects our spirituality and belief. For us, Jesus is the centre of our prayer life as he directs our thoughts and actions to God our Father. We pray in the power of the Holy Spirit.

The special emphasis we give in our prayers reflects the particular Christian Church to which we belong. The Eastern Church, for example, highlights the 'otherness' of God by its emphasis on the Holy Spirit as the great sanctifying force in our lives. The Church of England has a very strong establishment influence in its set prayers, while non-conformist Churches tend towards a more spontaneous form of open prayer. Roman Catholic spirituality, on the other hand, while not excluding any of these elements in its prayer life, lays great emphasis on the devotional aspect of our prayerful relationship with God.

Catholic prayer books, with their well-thumbed pages, were the treasured possession of Catholics for centuries. A prayer book given as a present to mark a special occasion, such as first communion, confirmation, or marriage, remained with the Catholic all through life. It represented part of his or her heritage. These prayer books were interlaced with special prayer cards, of personal spiritual significance to the owner, which told the story of his life and pilgrimage as a Christian. In one sense they were as revered by the Catholic as the Bible by a Protestant.

As Catholics today we are in danger of losing much

of what is best and beautiful in our spirituality. This is due indeliberately in large part to the Second Vatican Council with its emphasis on the need for renewal and relevance in Catholic teaching and practice. This bad side-effect of ignoring, or even rejecting, traditional Catholic prayers was not the Council's intention, but it was in fact what happened.

In a desire to update Catholic spirituality, and bring it into line with the new ecumenical thinking, there was a tendency for contemporary Catholic prayer books to pay scant, if any, attention to the prayers of a former age. These new prayer books were not only not Catholic prayer books as we knew them, but were scarcely distinguishable from other prayer books, even those not specifically Christian. Their main criterion was that authentic prayer must come from present-day life. In the process many of our beautiful old prayers, hallowed by use, were discarded. The fact that they had sustained countless millions in their spiritual lives was ignored, and thus many hallowed Catholic practices fell by the wayside. It is in an attempt to redress the balance that *The Catholic Prayer Book* has been compiled.

Because spirituality is an ongoing process the prayer book contains, we hope, a selection of the best contemporary prayers which will probably stand the test of time. Many old prayers, which are of great intrinsic spiritual value, have had to be updated because their over-ornate manner of expression tended to cloud their true meaning for us today.

In the heat of the Reformation, too, there was a tendency to overstress some aspects of Catholic doctrine and spirituality so that we could be clearly distinguished from our separated brethren. This difference has not been diluted, but has been placed in its true setting, either by the use of contemporary language, or a less strident proclamation of our belief. The adaptation of the prayers has been lit up by the Church's teaching on the resurrection, and the power of the Holy Spirit constantly at work in the Church through all the ages including our own. Many beautiful old prayers, however, defy adaptation, and remain in their original form because they are so clearly the work of the Spirit. They trip off the tongue because we not only know them *by heart* but *in our hearts* as well. Some prayers have been specially composed to fit the mood of our spirituality in those sections which needed amplification. This gives a more complete and rounded effect so that each section dovetails into the rest.

The Church is spiritually one. In this it reflects the unity of the Trinity. But we live, in fact, in a fragmented Church and world. We believe that the Spirit pours out his gifts on all those in the Church who confess Jesus as Lord to the glory of the Father. *The Catholic Prayer Book*, therefore, in acknowledging this diversity of spiritual gifts of the Spirit to all the members of Christ's spiritual Church, incorporates in its pages many prayers of Christian denominations other than Catholic. We appreciate the Spirit at work in the lives of Christians through prayer. In this way the prayer book reflects our ecumenical age, and deepens our Catholic spirituality. When we pray together as Christians then we are taking the best possible steps on the road to unity.

Our awareness of the diversity of the gifts of the Spirit makes us acknowledge also that we still have a lot to learn in our pilgrimage as Catholics from other Christian heritages. We, therefore, approach the Father in prayer in a spirit of humility and wonder. Accordingly, we hope that other Christian Churches will use this prayer book, not only to gain a fuller awareness of our Catholic prayer life, but also to deepen their own. We have a common Father, one mediator, and the same Spirit at work in all of us. *The Catholic Prayer Book* is for all Christians and not just for Catholics.

How to use the Prayer Book

*Prayer is basically personal. It is as unique to each one of us
as our fingerprints. It is a one-to-one relationship with God
my loving Father, and is all about my life with him. So, in a
sense, it is impossible to write a book of prayers for someone
else. But however personal it may be, true Christian prayer
has certain basic common strands because it involves the
community from which no one is excluded.*

In the final analysis only the Spirit of God can teach
us how to pray, or give us the words in which to express
our needs and deepest spiritual feelings (Romans
8:26-27). He prays in and through us. Without him we
cannot pray. How each individual uses this prayer
book depends on his or her unique situation, and present
relationship with God and the community. No hard or
fast set of rules can be laid down because we are dealing
with matters of the Spirit.

In prayer we live the life of the Blessed Trinity. It is
for this reason that the prayer book begins with a
section on prayers to the Father, Son and Holy Spirit.
This sets the tone of our spirituality, and our Christian
vocation. Catholic devotion is centred on the
sacraments which are our personal encounter with
Christ. The keystone of our worship is the eucharist in
which Christ is both our victim and spiritual food. The
prayers set out in this book help us to live out more
fully our sacramental life and worship. The final section
contains prayers for every aspect of our Christian
lives so that at all times and circumstances we live in
the presence of God the Father, Son and Holy Spirit.

The prayer book will afford us starting-off points for individual or group prayer. Just as a plane, to be airborne, needs a launching pad, so also this prayer book may help to lead us into prayerful conversation with God. It is a means to an end. The end is to be with God, especially in praise and thanksgiving.

Just as there are times spent in *talking* so there are also times for *listening* to God in prayer. What he says to us is much more important than what we say to him. Prayer is not a matter of talking a great deal but of loving a great deal. It is thinking about God while loving him, and loving him while thinking about him. Silence, for the Christian, is not just the absence of speech but the stillness of soul in which our true self is united with its creator and Father. We become silent in awe and wonder, as we contemplate God within us. It is an experience too rich and sensitive for words. But because we are human we use words and this is where *The Catholic Prayer Book* meets a need. We can use its formal prayers at any time of day or event in our lives because everything we do comes under the influence of prayer. We may choose to develop our awareness of God's presence, as a Father to us, with a few general prayers (p. 135) together with some morning prayers (p. 139). This may lead us into praise of God the Father (p. 3), to some devotion to Jesus our Saviour (p. 19) or to imploring the help and guidance in our lives of the Holy Spirit (p. 44).

We may wish to pray for a particular need of our world and community (p. 182), for someone who is ill (p. 223) or for some spiritual need for ourselves (p. 206). We may desire to consecrate the day and our lives to God (p. 139) or to implore the assistance of Our Lady (p. 235), the angels and saints (p. 252). A favourite litany or a phrase from it or any prayer from the prayer book, which has a special significance for us, may help to put our day in focus so that our waking hours are shot through with the light of God's love.

If we have a few quiet moments during the day then we can develop our spiritual awareness of God by saying one of the following, the Jesus Psalter (p. 19), the Jesus Prayer (p. 173), Devotion to the Five Sacred Wounds (p. 40), The Thirty Days Prayer (p. 241), the Bona Mors (p. 267), or any devotion which deepens our commitment through Christ to God our Father. Favourite Catholic devotions, like the Stations of the Cross (p. 33) or the Rosary (p. 245), have been of immense spiritual benefit in the lives of countless Catholics down through the ages. They were spiritually fed on litanies, novenas and the prayers of the saints. They are part of our treasure house of Catholic spirituality.

We are a sacramental people. In *The Catholic Prayer Book,* the section on the sacraments, especially the Mass, brings back many prayers hallowed throughout the ages. In this way the Catholic is plunged ever deeper into the personal life of Christ in his surrender to the Father. The Mass is the centre of our lives. We can recall its power during the day by saying the prayers before and after Mass (pp. 61/94), before and after communion (pp. 96/102), or prayers before the Blessed Sacrament (p. 105). We are aware of God's mercy to us in the sacrament of reconciliation (p. 122) and of our rebirth as Christians in the sacrament of baptism (p. 55). Finally, at the evening's close, we have special prayers (p. 155) and prayers of the Spirit (p. 160).

The manner in which each person uses *The Catholic Prayer Book* will be unique as he or she grows in the life of the Spirit. He will come to love and treasure it as an instrument that has led to a fuller life with God. This is its function and my prayer for you.

MICHAEL BUCKLEY

The Christian Vocation

Christ was intended by God the Father, from the very beginning, to be the crowning point and purpose of creation. He *is the image of the unseen God and the first-born of all creation*, Colossians 1:15. He is the centre in which the human capacity for union with God is to be fully realised: *God wanted all perfection to be found in him*, Colossians 1:19. We were to share the life of the Son, and to come to the Father through him. We were to be sons of God and possess his Spirit. Such was God's purpose for us. This was our destiny.

However, God created man free. In his freedom man created a sin-filled history. Humanity had become a fallen race. It needed to be redeemed and restored to its former destiny. It is into this sin-filled world that *when the appointed time came, God sent his Son, born of a woman, born a subject of the Law, to redeem the subjects of the Law and to enable us to be adopted as sons*, Galatians 4:4–6. Christ is the restorer of man's dignity and destiny.

The testimony of the Son to the Father, given in the conditions of this fallen world, was manifested in his perfect obedience to his Father's will even to death on a cross. The life and death of the Son reveal God the Father as a saving God whose love overcomes man's sinfulness: *God loved the world so much that he gave his only Son, so that everyone who believes in him may not be lost but may have eternal life,* John 3:16. The Father responds to his Son's perfect love and obedience by raising him from the dead and setting him at his right hand in glory. The humiliated servant is revealed as the Lord of Glory whose destiny we now share.

In Christ a new age is established. He has conquered sin, death and the world and has passed to his heavenly existence, where he awaits those who believe in him. He will come again at the final consummation of all things and in him the fall and rise of creation will find its true meaning. As Christians we are a new creation. We are an Easter people whose praise of God is rooted in the resurrection.

God's original plan of uniting all mankind to himself is now being fulfilled in Christ's Church, or community of believers. Just as the Father chose a people, the Israelites, to proclaim his presence and love in the world, so now the Church, Christ's body on earth, proclaims the loving Fatherhood of God in his risen Son. To enable us to do this Christ sends his Holy Spirit to us: *Everyone moved by the Spirit is a son of God. The spirit you received is not the spirit of slaves bringing fear into your lives again; it is the spirit of sons, and it makes us cry out, 'Abba, Father!'* Romans 8:14–16. The Christian life is, therefore, the life of the blessed Trinity. Created by the Father, redeemed by the Son, and sanctified by the Holy Spirit, we live out our destiny in the Church and world through prayer and the sacraments. This is our Christian vocation.

Prayers to God the Father

*God is our Father to whom all prayer is directed. We were
made to know, love and serve him. Every gift comes from him
as its source and returns to him as its final end. We praise
and adore him for all the gifts of creation, but especially for
the gift of his only Son by whom we are redeemed.*

Thanksgiving and praise for Creation, Faith and Salvation
A general thanksgiving

Lord, open my lips, and my mouth shall proclaim your
praise. To you be glory in the Church and in Christ
Jesus
from generation to generation evermore.

Almighty God, of all mercies, Father,
we, your unworthy servants,
give you most humble and hearty thanks
for all your goodness and loving kindness
to us and to all men.

We bless you for our creation, preservation,
and all the blessings of this life.

But, above all, we thank you for your infinite love
in the redemption of the world by our Lord Jesus
Christ,
for the means of grace and the hope of glory.

And, we pray, give us a due sense of all your mercies,
that our hearts may be truly thankful,
and that we may declare your praise

3

not only with our lips but in our lives,
by giving ourselves to your service
and by walking before you in holiness and
righteousness all our days;

Through Jesus Christ our Lord,
to whom, with you and the Holy Spirit,
be all honour and glory world without end.

Alleluia!
Give thanks to the Lord, for he is good,
    his love is everlasting!
Give thanks to the God of gods,
    his love is everlasting!
Give thanks to the Lord of lords,
    his love is everlasting!

He alone performs great marvels,
    his love is everlasting!
His wisdom made the heavens,
    his love is everlasting!
He set the earth on the waters,
    his love is everlasting!

He made the great lights,
    his love is everlasting!
The sun to govern the day,
    his love is everlasting!
Moon and stars to govern the night,
    his love is everlasting!

He provides for all living creatures,
    his love is everlasting!
Give thanks to the God of Heaven,
    his love is everlasting!

Psalm 136

Thanksgiving for creation
Thanks be to God for the light and the darkness;
Thanks be to God for the hail and the snow;
Thanks be to God for shower and sunshine;
Thanks be to God for all things that grow;
Thanks be to God for lightning and tempests;
Thanks be to God for weal and woe;
Thanks be to God for his own great goodness;
Thanks be to God for what is, is so;
Thanks be to God when the harvest is plenty;
Thanks be to God when the barn is low;
Thanks be to God when our pockets are empty;
Thanks be to God when again they o'erflow.

How great is your name, O Lord our God,
through all the earth!
Your majesty is praised above the heavens;
on the lips of children and on babes
you have found praise to foil your enemy,
to silence the foe and the rebel.

When I see the heavens, the work of your hands,
the moon and the stars which you arranged,
what is man that you should keep him in mind,
mortal man that you care for him?

You have made him little less than a god;
with glory and honour you crowned him,
gave him power over the works of your hand,
put all things under his feet.

All of them, sheep and cattle,
yes, even the savage beasts,
birds of the air, and fish
that make their way through the waters.

How great is your name, O Lord our God,
through all the earth!

Psalm 8

I offer thee
Every flower that ever grew,
Every bird that ever flew,
Every wind that ever blew.

Good God!

Every thunder rolling,
Every church bell tolling,
Every leaf and sod.

Laudamus Te!

I offer thee
Every wave that ever moved,
Every heart that ever loved,
Thee, thy Father's well-beloved.

Dear Lord!

Every river dashing,
Every lightning flashing,
Like an angel's sword.

Benedicimus Te!

I offer thee
Every cloud that ever swept
O'er the skies, and broke and wept
In rain, and with the flowerets slept.

My King!

Every communicant praying,
Every angel staying
Before thy throne to sing.

Adoramus Te!

I offer thee
Every flake of virgin snow,
Every spring of earth below,
Every human joy and woe.

     My love!

O Lord! And all thy glorious
Self o'er death victorious,
Throned in heaven above.

    Glorificamus Te!
    Ancient Irish Prayer

Praise in creation
Glory be to God for dappled things –
  For skies of couple-colour as a brinded cow;
    For rose-moles all in stipple upon trout that
swim;
Fresh-firecoal chestnut-falls; finches' wings;
  Landscape plotted and pieced – fold, fallow, and
plough;
    And áll trádes, their gear and tackle and trim.

All things counter, original, spare, strange;
  Whatever is fickle, freckled (who knows how?)
    With swift, slow; sweet, sour; adazzle, dim;
He fathers-forth whose beauty is past change:
    Praise him.

    Gerard Manley Hopkins

We praise Thee, O God, for Thy glory displayed in all
 the creatures of the earth,
In the snow, in the rain, in the wind, in the storm; in
 all of Thy creatures, both the hunters and the
 hunted.
For all things exist only as seen by Thee, only as
 known by Thee, all things exist

Only in Thy light, and Thy glory is declared even in
    that which denies Thee; the darkness declares the
    glory of light.
Those who deny Thee could not deny, if Thou didst
    not exist; and their denial is never complete, for if it
    were so, they would not exist.
They affirm Thee in living; all things affirm Thee in
    living; the bird in the air, both the hawk and the
    finch; the beast on the earth, both the wolf and the
    lamb; the worm in the soil and the worm in the belly.
Therefore man, whom Thou hast made to be conscious
    of Thee, must consciously praise Thee, in thought
    and in word and in deed.
Even with the hand to the broom, the back bent in
    laying the fire, the knee bent in cleaning the hearth,
    we, the scrubbers and sweepers of Canterbury,
The back bent under toil, the knee bent under sin, the
    hands to the face under fear, the head bent under
    grief,
Even in us the voices of seasons, the snuffle of winter,
    the song of spring, the drone of summer, the voices
    of beasts and of birds, praise Thee.
We thank Thee for Thy mercies of blood, for Thy
    redemption by blood. For the blood of Thy martyrs
    and saints
Shall enrich the earth, shall create the holy places.
For wherever a saint has dwelt, wherever a martyr has
    given his blood for the blood of Christ,
There is holy ground, and the sanctity shall not depart
    from it
Though armies trample over it, though sightseers
    come with guide-books looking over it;
From where the western seas gnaw at the coast of
    Iona,
To the death in the desert, the prayer in forgotten
    places by the broken imperial column,

From such ground springs that which forever renews
　　the earth
Though it is forever denied. Therefore, O God, we
　　thank Thee
Who hast given such blessing in Canterbury.

T. S. Eliot

Hymn of praise
Most high Lord,
Yours are the praises,
The glory and the honors,
And to you alone must be accorded
All graciousness; and no man there is
Who is worthy to name you.
Be praisèd, O God, and be exalted,
My Lord of all creatures,
And in especial of the most high Sun
Which is your creature, O Lord, that makes clear
The day and illumines it,
Whence by its fairness and its splendor
It is become thy face;
And of the white moon (be praised, O Lord)
And of the wandering stars,
Created by you in the heaven
So brilliant and so fair.
Praised be my Lord, by the flame
Whereby night groweth illumined
In the midst of its darkness,
For it is resplendent,
Is joyous, fair, eager; is mighty.
Praisèd be my Lord, of the air,
Of the winds, of the clear sky,
And of the cloudy, praisèd
Of all seasons whereby
Live all these creatures
Of lower order.

Praised be my Lord,
By our sister the water,
Element meetest for man,
Humble and chaste in its clearness.
Praised be the Lord by our mother
The Earth that sustaineth,
That feeds, that produceth
Multitudinous grasses
And flowers and fruitage.
Praised be my Lord, by those
Who grant pardons through his love,
Enduring their travail in patience
And their infirmity with joy of the spirit.
Praisèd be my Lord by death corporal
Whence escapes no one living.
Woe to those that die in mutual transgression
And blessed are they who shall
Find in death's hour thy grace that comes
From obedience to thy holy will,
Wherethrough they shall never see
The pain of the death eternal.
Praise and give grace to my Lord,
Be grateful and serve him
In humbleness e'en as ye are,
Praise him all creatures!

Saint Francis of Assisi, translated by Ezra Pound

Psalm praise
Praise, O servants of the Lord,
praise the name of the Lord!
May the name of the Lord be blessed
both now and for evermore!
From the rising of the sun to its setting
praised be the name of the Lord!

High above all nations is the Lord,
above the heavens his glory.
Who is like the Lord, our God,
who has risen on high to his throne
yet stoops from the heights to look down,
to look down upon heaven and earth?

From the dust he lifts up the lowly,
from the dungheap he raises the poor
to set him in the company of princes,
yes, with the princes of his people.
To the childless wife he gives a home
and gladdens her heart with children.

Psalm 112

Let the peoples praise you, O God;
let all the peoples praise you.

Let the nations be glad and exult
for you rule the world with justice.
With fairness you rule the peoples,
you guide the nations on earth.

Let the peoples praise you, O God;
let all the peoples praise you.

The earth has yielded its fruit
for God, our God, has blessed us.
May God still give us his blessing
till the ends of the earth revere him.

Let the peoples praise you, O God;
let all the peoples praise you.

Psalm 66

I thank you, Lord, with all my heart,
you have heard the words of my mouth.
Before the angels I will bless you.
I will adore before your holy temple.

I thank you for your faithfulness and love
which excel all we ever knew of you.
On the day I called, you answered;
you increased the strength of my soul.

All earth's kings shall thank you
when they hear the words of your mouth.
They shall sing of the Lord's ways:
'How great is the glory of the Lord!'

The Lord is high yet he looks on the lowly
and the haughty he knows from afar.
Though I walk in the midst of affliction
you give me life and frustrate my foes.

You stretch out your hand and save me,
your hand will do all things for me.
Your love, O Lord, is eternal,
discard not the work of your hands.

Psalm 137

I will praise you, Lord, you have rescued me
and have not let my enemies rejoice over me.

O Lord, I cried to you for help
and you, my God, have healed me.
O Lord, you have raised my soul from the dead,
restored me to life from those who sink into the grave.

Sing psalms to the Lord, you who love him,
give thanks to his holy name.

His anger lasts but a moment; his favour through life.
At night there are tears, but joy comes with dawn.

I said to myself in my good fortune:
'Nothing will ever disturb me.'
Your favour had set me on a mountain fastness,
then you hid your face and I was put to confusion.

To you, Lord, I cried,
to my God I made appeal:
'What profit would my death be, my going to the
grave?
Can dust give you praise or proclaim your truth?'

The Lord listened and had pity.
The Lord came to my help.
For me you have changed my mourning into dancing,
you removed my sackcloth and girdled me with joy.
So my soul sings psalms to you unceasingly.
O Lord my God, I will thank you for ever.

Psalm 29

I will give you glory, O God my King,
I will bless your name for ever.

I will bless you day after day
and praise your name for ever.
The Lord is great, highly to be praised,
his greatness cannot be measured.

Age to age shall proclaim your works,
shall declare your mighty deeds,
shall speak of your splendour and glory,
tell the tale of your wonderful works.

They will speak of your terrible deeds,
recount your greatness and might.
They will recall your abundant goodness;
age to age shall ring out your justice.

The Lord is kind and full of compassion,
slow to anger, abounding in love.
How good is the Lord to all,
compassionate to all his creatures.

All your creatures shall thank you, O Lord,
and your friends shall repeat their blessing.
They shall speak of the glory of your reign
and declare your might, O God,

to make known to men your mighty deeds
and the glorious splendour of your reign.
Yours is an everlasting kingdom;
your rule lasts from age to age.

The Lord is faithful in all his words
and loving in all his deeds.
The Lord supports all who fall
and raises all who are bowed down.

The eyes of all creatures look to you
and you give them their food in due time.
You open wide your hand,
grant the desires of all who live.

The Lord is just in all his ways
and loving in all his deeds.
He is close to all who call him,
who call on him from their hearts.

He grants the desires of those who fear him,
he hears their cry and he saves them.
The Lord protects all who love him;
but the wicked he will utterly destroy.

Let me speak the praise of the Lord,
let all mankind bless his holy name
for ever, for ages unending.

Psalm 144

Praise and Thanksgiving
O Light Invisible, we praise Thee!
Too bright for mortal vision.
O Greater Light, we praise Thee for the less;
The eastern light our spires touch at morning,
The light that slants upon our western doors at
evening,
The twilight over stagnant pools at batflight,
Moon light and star light, owl and moth light,
Glow-worm glowlight on a grassblade.
O Light Invisible, we worship Thee!

We thank Thee for the lights that we have kindled,
The light of altar and of sanctuary;
Small lights of those who meditate at midnight
And lights directed through the coloured panes of
windows
And light reflected from the polished stone,
The gilded carven wood, the coloured fresco.
Our gaze is submarine, our eyes look upward
And see the light that fractures through unquiet water.
We see the light but see not whence it comes.
O Light Invisible, we glorify Thee.

T. S. Eliot

Praise to the holiest in the height,
And in the depth be praise:
In all his words most wonderful;
Most sure in all his ways!

O loving wisdom of our God!
When all was sin and shame,
A second Adam to the fight
And to the rescue came.

O wisest love! that flesh and blood
Which did in Adam fail,
Should strive afresh against the foe,
Should strive and should prevail.

And that a higher gift than grace
Should flesh and blood refine,
God's presence and his very self,
And essence all divine.

O generous love! that he who smote
In man for man the foe,
The double agony in man
For man should undergo;

And in the garden secretly,
And on the cross on high,
Should teach his brethren and inspire
To suffer and to die.

John Henry Newman

Magnificat
My soul glorifies the Lord,
my spirit rejoices in God, my Saviour.
He looks on his servant in her nothingness;
henceforth all ages will call me blessed.

The Almighty works marvels for me.
Holy his name!
His mercy is from age to age,
on those who fear him.
He puts forth his arm in strength
and scatters the mighty from their thrones
and raises the lowly.
He fills the starving with good things,
sends the rich away empty.
He protects Israel his servant,
remembering his mercy,
the mercy promised to our fathers,
for Abraham and his sons for ever.

Luke 1:46–55

Thanksgiving for salvation
He is the image of the unseen God
and the first-born of all creation,
for in him were created
all things in heaven and on earth:
everything visible and everything invisible,
Thrones, Dominations, Sovereignties, Powers –
all things were created through him and for him.
Before anything was created, he existed,
and he holds all things in unity.
Now the Church is his body,
he is its head.

As he is the Beginning,
he was first to be born from the dead,
so that he should be first in every way;
because God wanted all perfection
to be found in him
and all things to be reconciled through him
and for him,

everything in heaven and everything on earth,
when he made peace
by his death on the cross.

Colossians 1:15–20

Infinite God, the brightness of whose face is often
hidden from my mortal gaze,
I thank you that you sent your Son,
Jesus Christ, to be a light in a dark world.
I thank you Christ, light of light, that in your most holy
life you pierced the eternal mystery as with a great
shaft of light,
so that on seeing you we see him whom no one has
ever seen.

John Baillie*

Lord of all life, we praise you, that through Christ's
resurrection, the old order of sin and death is
overcome and all things made new in him: grant that
being dead to sin we may live to you in newness of life
through Jesus Christ, Our Lord.

Thanksgiving for the gift of faith
My God, from my heart I thank you for the many
blessings you have given me. I thank you for having
created and baptised me, for having placed me in your
holy Catholic Church, and for having given me so
many graces and mercies through the merits of Jesus
Christ. I thank your Son Jesus, for having died upon
the cross that I might receive pardon for my sins and
obtain my eternal salvation. I thank you for all your
other mercies you have given me through Jesus Christ,
Our Lord.

Prayers to God the Son

Jesus came that we might share his risen life. He is one with the Father. The Christian life is a communion of love joining us with God and with each other. Christ is the centre of the circle, the hour glass through which our lives flow in prayer in order to be purified from the effects of sin. All our prayer, by the power of his Spirit, is directed to the Father through Christ's risen life at work in us. We are a resurrection people and 'alleluia' is our song.

Jesus Psalter

The Psalter is made up of three parts, each part consisting of five petitions. Each petition is followed by the prayers 'Have mercy on all sinners, Jesus, I beseech you . . .' and 'O blessed Trinity . . .' The fifth, tenth and fifteenth petitions, which bring the three parts to a close, conclude with 'He was humbler yet . . .'; 'Hear these my petitions . . .', and 'I believe in God . . .'

PART ONE

Begin by kneeling devoutly, or bowing, at the adorable name of JESUS, saying:
In the heavens, on earth and in the underworld,
all should bend the knee at the name of Jesus
and every tongue should acclaim
Jesus Christ as Lord,
to the glory of God the Father.

Philippians 2:10–11

FIRST PETITION

Jesus, Jesus, Jesus,
Jesus, Jesus, Jesus, } have mercy on me.
Jesus, Jesus, Jesus,

Jesus, have mercy on me, O God of compassion, and forgive the many and great offences which I have committed in your sight.

Many have been the follies of my life, and great are the miseries which I have deserved for my ingratitude.

Have mercy on me, dear Jesus, for I am weak;

O Lord, heal me, who am unable to help myself.

Deliver me from setting my heart upon any of your creatures, which may divert my eyes from a continual looking up to you.

Grant me grace henceforth, for the love of you, to hate sin; and out of a just esteem of you, to despise all worldly vanities.

Have mercy on all sinners, Jesus, I beseech you; turn their vices into virtues; and, making them true observers of your law and sincere lovers of you, bring them to bliss in everlasting glory.

Have mercy also on the souls in purgatory, for your bitter passion, I beseech you, and for your glorious name, Jesus.

O blessed Trinity, one eternal God, have mercy on me.

Our Father.   Hail Mary.

SECOND PETITION

Jesus, Jesus, Jesus,
Jesus, Jesus, Jesus, } help me.
Jesus, Jesus, Jesus,

Jesus, help me to overcome all temptations to sin, and the malice of my spiritual enemy.

Help me to spend my time in virtuous actions, and in such labours as are acceptable to you.

Help me to resist and repel the inclinations of my flesh to sloth, gluttony, and impurity.

Help me to make my heart be attracted by virtue, and inflamed with desires of your glorious presence.

Help me to deserve and keep a good name, by a peaceful and holy living; to your honour, O Jesus, to my own peace, and the benefit of others.

Have mercy . . .   O blessed Trinity . . .
Our Father.   Hail Mary.

THIRD PETITION

      Jesus, Jesus, Jesus, ⎞
      Jesus, Jesus, Jesus, ⎬   strengthen me.
      Jesus, Jesus, Jesus, ⎠

Jesus, strengthen me in soul and body, to please you in doing such works of virtue as may bring me to your everlasting joy and happiness.

Grant me a firm purpose, most merciful Saviour, to amend my life, and to compensate for the years past: Those years which I have misspent in vain or wicked thoughts, words, deeds, and evil habits.

Make my heart obedient to your will, and ready, for your love, to perform all the works of mercy.

Grant me the gifts of the Holy Spirit, which by a virtuous life, and devout frequenting of your most holy sacraments, will bring me to your heavenly kingdom.

Have mercy . . .   O blessed Trinity . . .
Our Father.   Hail Mary.

FOURTH PETITION

      Jesus, Jesus, Jesus, ⎞
      Jesus, Jesus, Jesus, ⎬   comfort me.
      Jesus, Jesus, Jesus, ⎠

Jesus, comfort me, and give me grace to place my chief, my only joy and happiness in you.

Give me the grace of contemplative prayer, inner

peace and a fervent desire of your glory; fill my soul with the contemplation of heaven, that I may dwell there everlastingly with you.

Bring often to my remembrance your unsurpassable goodness, your gifts, and the great kindness which you have shown me.

And when you bring to my mind the sad remembrance of my sins, whereby I have so ungratefully offended you, comfort me with the assurance of obtaining your grace by the spirit of perfect repentance, which will take away my guilt, and prepare me for your kingdom.

Have mercy . . .   O blessed Trinity . . .
Our Father.   Hail Mary.

FIFTH PETITION

> Jesus, Jesus, Jesus, ⎫
> Jesus, Jesus, Jesus, ⎬   make me constant.
> Jesus, Jesus, Jesus, ⎭

Jesus, make me constant in faith, hope, and charity; and give me perseverance in all virtues, and a resolution never to offend you.

Let the memory of your passion, and of those bitter pains you suffered for me, strengthen my patience, and defend me in all tribulation and adversity.

Let me always hold fast to the doctrines of your Catholic Church, and fulfil all my Christian obligations.

Let no false delight of this deceitful world blind me, no temptation of the flesh or fraud of the devil, shake my heart:

My heart, which seeks you for its eternal rest and resolves to seek your eternal reward above all else.

Have mercy . . .   O blessed Trinity . . .

He was humbler yet, even to accepting death, death on a cross.

Philippians 2:8

Hear these my petitions, O most merciful Saviour, and grant me grace to repeat and consider them frequently so that they may prove easy steps whereby my soul may ascend to the knowledge, love, and performance of my duty to you, and my neighbour, through the whole course of my life. Amen.
Our Father. Hail Mary. I believe in God . . .

PART TWO
Begin as before, saying: 'In the heavens, on earth . . .'

SIXTH PETITION
Jesus, Jesus, Jesus,
Jesus, Jesus, Jesus,   enlighten me with
Jesus, Jesus, Jesus,   spiritual wisdom.

Jesus, enlighten me with spiritual wisdom to know your goodness, and all those things which are most acceptable to you.
Grant me a clear understanding of my only good, and wisdom to order my life according to it.
Grant that I may grow in virtue, till at length I arrive at the clear vision of your glorious majesty.
Permit me not, dear Lord, to return to those sins for which I have been sorry, and which I have confessed and done penance for.
Grant me grace to benefit the souls of others by my good example, and to win back, by good counsel, those who offend against me.
Have mercy . . . O blessed Trinity . . .
Our Father. Hail Mary.

SEVENTH PETITION
Jesus, Jesus, Jesus,
Jesus, Jesus, Jesus,   grant me grace
Jesus, Jesus, Jesus,   to fear you.

Jesus, grant me grace inwardly to fear losing your friendship and to avoid all occasions of offending you. Let your warning of the punishments which are to fall on sinners, the fear of losing your love, and your heavenly inheritance, always keep me in awe.

Let me not risk losing your friendship by sin, but soon return to repentance, lest the sentence of endless death and damnation fall upon me.

Let the powerful intercession of your Blessed Mother, and all your saints, but above all, your own merits and mercy, O my Saviour, be ever between your righteous justice and my soul still tempted by sin.

Enable me, O my God, to work out my salvation with fear and trembling; and let the understanding of your secret judgments render me a more humble and diligent lover at the throne of your grace.

Have mercy . . . O blessed Trinity . . .
Our Father. Hail Mary.

EIGHTH PETITION

Jesus, Jesus, Jesus,
Jesus, Jesus, Jesus, } grant me grace
Jesus, Jesus, Jesus, to love you.

Jesus, grant me grace truly to love you for your infinite goodness, and for the wonderful bounties which I have received, and hope for ever to receive from you.

Let the remembrance of your kindness and patience conquer the malice and wretched inclinations of my fallen nature.

Let the consideration of my many deliverances, your frequent graces, and continual assistance in my life, make me ashamed of my ingratitude.

You grant me all your mercies, so that I may love you as my only good.

O my dear Lord, my whole life shall be nothing but a desire of you; and because I indeed love you, I will

24

most lovingly keep your commandments.
Have mercy . . .   O blessed Trinity . . .
Our Father.   Hail Mary.

NINTH PETITION
>   Jesus, Jesus, Jesus,⎫   grant me grace
>   Jesus, Jesus, Jesus,⎬   to remember
>   Jesus, Jesus, Jesus,⎭   my death.

Jesus, grant me grace always to remember my death,
and the account which I am then to give, so that my
soul, being always well disposed, may depart out of
this world in your grace.
Then, by the holy intercession of your Blessed Mother
and Saint Joseph, and the assistance of the glorious
Saint Michael, deliver me from the enemy of my soul;
and do you, my good angel, I beseech you, help me at
that most solemn hour.
Then, dear Jesus, remember your mercy, and turn not
your most lovable face away from me because of my
offences.
Prepare me for that day, by causing me now to die
daily to all earthly things, and so to have my
conversation continually in heaven.
Let the remembrance of my death teach me how to
esteem my life; and the memory of your resurrection
encourage me to meet my death with cheerfulness.
Have mercy . . .   O blessed Trinity . . .
Our Father.   Hail Mary.

TENTH PETITION
>   Jesus, Jesus, Jesus,⎫
>   Jesus, Jesus, Jesus,⎬   send me here
>   Jesus, Jesus, Jesus,⎭   my purgatory.

Jesus, send me here my purgatory, so that I may be
made ready to share the happiness of heaven.
Grant me those merciful crosses and afflictions which

take away my false affection for all things here below.
Since no one can see you that loves anything which is
not for your sake, suffer not my heart to find any rest
here, but in you alone.

Grant that I may never suffer from the anguish of a
soul that is separated from you, that desires, but
cannot come to you because of sin.

Keep me continually mortified to this world, that being
thoroughly purified by the fire of your love, I may
immediately pass from this life into your everlasting
kingdom.

Have mercy . . .   O blessed Trinity . . .

He was humbler yet, even to accepting death, death on a
cross.

Philippians 2:8

Hear these my petitions, O my most merciful Saviour,
and grant me grace to repeat and consider them
frequently so that they may prove easy steps whereby
my soul may ascend to the knowledge, love and
performance of my duty to you, and my neighbour,
through the whole course of my life. Amen.

Our Father.   Hail Mary.   I believe in God . . .

PART THREE
Begin as before, saying: *In the heavens, on earth . . .*

ELEVENTH PETITION

> Jesus, Jesus, Jesus,
> Jesus, Jesus, Jesus,   help me in my
> Jesus, Jesus, Jesus,   human relationships.

Jesus, help me in my human relationships so that I
may always see you in the other person.

Cause me, O blessed Lord, to remember always, that
you are present to all our words and actions. May I
always speak the truth in charity and never hurt my

neighbour by speaking evil of him when it is better to be silent.

Control in me, dear Jesus, all inordinate affections to things of the flesh so that I treat other people with love and respect.

Your power defend, your wisdom direct, your fatherly pity correct me, and make me so live here among people, that I may be fit for the conversation of angels hereafter.

Have mercy . . .   O blessed Trinity . . .
Our Father.   Hail Mary.

TWELFTH PETITION

Jesus, Jesus, Jesus,⎫   grant me grace
Jesus, Jesus, Jesus,⎬   to call on you
Jesus, Jesus, Jesus,⎭   for help.

Jesus, grant me grace in all my needs to call on you for help, faithfully remembering your death and resurrection for my sake.

You will listen to my cries, because you laid down your life for my ransom and you will save me because you took it up again for your crown.

You intercede for me in heaven because you have promised: 'Call upon me in the day of trouble, and I will deliver you'.

You are my sure rock of defence against all sorts of enemies; you are my ever-present grace, able to strengthen me to every good work.

Therefore, in all my sufferings, weaknesses and temptations, I will confidently call on you; hear me, O my Jesus, and when you hear, have mercy.

Have mercy . . .   O blessed Trinity . . .
Our Father.   Hail Mary.

Jesus, Jesus, Jesus,
Jesus, Jesus, Jesus, } make me persevere
Jesus, Jesus, Jesus, in virtue.

Jesus, make me persevere in virtue and a good life, and never fail in your service, till you bring me to my place in your kingdom.

In every aspect of my work and prayer strengthen, O Lord, my soul and body. May I see life as a pilgrimage on earth towards the new Jerusalem, a journey which I must constantly pursue without turning from the true path. O Jesus, make me always consider your blessed example: through how much pain, you pressed on to a bitter death, your way to a glorious resurrection.

Make me, O my redeemer, seriously weigh your words, 'He that perseveres to the end shall be saved'.

Have mercy . . .   O blessed Trinity . . .
Our Father.   Hail Mary.

Jesus, Jesus, Jesus, } grant me grace
Jesus, Jesus, Jesus, } to fix my
Jesus, Jesus, Jesus, } mind on you.

Jesus, grant me grace to fix my mind on you, especially in time of prayer, when I directly converse with you. Stop the wanderings of my mind, and the desires of my fickle heart; suppress the power of my spiritual enemies, who endeavour at that time to draw me from thinking of and loving you.

So shall I, with joy and gratitude, look on you as my deliverer from all the evils I have escaped; and as my benefactor for all the good I have ever received, or can hope for.

I shall see that you are my only good, and that all other things are but means, ordained by you, to make me fix my mind on you, to make me love you more and more,

and, by loving you, to be eternally happy.
O beloved of my soul, sanctify all my thoughts on earth that my eyes may become worthy to behold you face to face in your glory for ever.
Have mercy . . .   O blessed Trinity . . .
Our Father.   Hail Mary.

FIFTEENTH PETITION

Jesus, Jesus, Jesus,⎫ give me grace to order
Jesus, Jesus, Jesus, ⎬ my life towards my
Jesus, Jesus, Jesus,⎭ eternal happiness.

Jesus, give me grace to order my life towards my eternal happiness; so that all the actions of my body and soul may fit me for eternal happiness with you. May I see this world as a place in which we live in order to fit us for the next by desiring God as our only end.

Break my proud spirit, O Jesus; make it humble and obedient: grant me grace to depart this life with a heart filled with joy at my going to you.

Let the memory of your passion make me cheerfully undergo all temptations or sufferings here for your love, while my soul longs for that blissful life and immortal glory, which you have prepared in heaven for your servants.

O Jesus, let me frequently and attentively consider, that whatever I gain, if I lose you, all is lost; and whatever I lose, if I gain you, all is gained.

Have Mercy . . .   O blessed Trinity . . .

He was humbler yet, even to accepting death, death on a cross.

Philippians 2:8

Hear these my petitions, O my most merciful Saviour, and grant me grace so frequently to repeat and consider them that they may prove easy steps whereby

29

my soul may ascend to the knowledge, love, and
performance of my duty to you, and my neighbour,
through the whole course of my life. Amen.
Our Father.   Hail Mary.   I believe in God.

The Litany of the Sacred Heart

Lord, have mercy on us. **Lord have mercy on us.**
Christ, have mercy on us. **Christ, have mercy on us.**
Lord, have mercy on us. **Lord, have mercy on us.**
Christ, hear us.   **Christ, graciously hear us.**
God the Father of heaven,
                         have mercy on us.
God the Son, redeemer of the world,
                         have mercy on us.
God the Holy Spirit,   **have mercy on us.**
Holy Trinity one God,   **have mercy on us.**
Heart of Jesus, Son of the eternal Father,
                         have mercy on us.
Heart of Jesus, formed by the Holy Spirit in the womb
    of the virgin mother,   **have mercy on us.**
Heart of Jesus, wonderfully united to the eternal word,
                         have mercy on us.
Heart of Jesus, of infinite majesty,
                         have mercy on us.
Heart of Jesus, holy temple of God,
                         have mercy on us.
Heart of Jesus, tabernacle of the most high,
                         have mercy on us.
Heart of Jesus, house of God and gate of heaven,
                         have mercy on us.
Heart of Jesus, burning furnace of charity,
                         have mercy on us.
Heart of Jesus, vessel of justice and love,
                         have mercy on us.
Heart of Jesus, never-ending source of all virtues,
                         have mercy on us.

Heart of Jesus, worthy of all praise,
>**have mercy on us.**

Heart of Jesus, king and centre of all hearts,
>**have mercy on us.**

Heart of Jesus, in which are all the treasures of wisdom and knowledge, >**have mercy on us.**

Heart of Jesus, in which dwells all the fullness of the divinity, >**have mercy on us.**

Heart of Jesus, in which the Father is well pleased,
>**have mercy on us.**

Heart of Jesus, of whose fullness we have all received,
>**have mercy on us.**

Heart of Jesus, deepest desire of the human heart,
>**have mercy on us.**

Heart of Jesus, patient and abounding in mercy,
>**have mercy on us.**

Heart of Jesus, generous to all who call upon you,
>**have mercy on us.**

Heart of Jesus, fountain of life and holiness,
>**have mercy on us.**

Heart of Jesus, atonement for our sins,
>**have mercy on us.**

Heart of Jesus, which suffered rejection for our sake,
>**have mercy on us.**

Heart of Jesus, bruised for our sins,
>**have mercy on us.**

Heart of Jesus, made obedient unto death,
>**have mercy on us.**

Heart of Jesus, pierced with a lance,
>**have mercy on us.**

Heart of Jesus, source of all consolation,
>**have mercy on us.**

Heart of Jesus, our peace and reconciliation,
>**have mercy on us.**

Heart of Jesus, victim of our sins,
>**have mercy on us.**

Heart of Jesus, salvation of those who hope in you,
have mercy on us.
Heart of Jesus, hope of those who die in you,
have mercy on us.
Heart of Jesus, our light and resurrection,
have mercy on us.
Heart of Jesus, delight of all the saints,
have mercy on us.
Lamb of God, you take away the sins of the world,
spare us, O Lord.
Lamb of God, you take away the sins of the world,
graciously hear us, O Lord.
Lamb of God, you take away the sins of the world,
have mercy on us.
Jesus, meek and humble of heart,
make our hearts like unto yours.

Let us pray.
Almighty and eternal God, look upon the heart of your well-loved Son and the praises and sacrifice he offers you in the name of sinners; being pleased with his holy obedience, pardon those who implore your mercy and give us a share in his resurrection, in the name of the same Jesus Christ your Son who lives and reigns with you in the unity of the Holy Spirit, one God for ever and ever. **Amen.**

The Way of the Cross

Jesus Christ, my Lord, with what great love you passed over the painful road which led you to death; and I, how often have I abandoned you. But now I love you with my whole soul, and because I love you, I am sincerely sorry for having offended you. My Jesus, pardon me, and permit me to accompany you in this journey. You are going to die for love of me, and it is my wish also, my dearest redeemer, to die for love of you.

Jesus, in your love I wish to live, in your love I wish to die.

FIRST STATION

Jesus is condemned to death

This response is said before each station.
We adore you, Christ, and praise you.
Because by your holy cross you have redeemed the world.

> Consider how Jesus, after having been scourged and crowned with thorns, was unjustly condemned by Pilate to die on the cross.

My loving Jesus, it was not Pilate; no, it was my sins that condemned you to die. I beseech you, by the merits of this sorrowful journey, to assist my soul in her journey towards eternity.

The following prayers and verse are said after each station.

I love you Jesus, my love, above all things;
I repent with my whole heart for having offended you.
Never permit me to separate myself from you again.

Grant that I may love you always,
then do with me what you will.
Our Father. Hail Mary. Glory be to the Father.

Jesus receives the cross

We adore . . .

> Consider how Jesus, in making this journey
> with the cross on his shoulders, thought of us,
> and offered for us to his Father the death he was
> about to undergo.

My most beloved Jesus, I embrace all the tribulations
you have destined for me until death. I beseech you by
the merits of the pain you suffered in carrying your
cross, to give me the necessary help to carry mine with
perfect patience and resignation.

I love you Jesus . . . Our Father. Hail Mary. Glory be.

Jesus falls the first time

We adore . . .

> Consider the first fall of Jesus under his cross.
> His flesh was torn by the scourges, his head was
> crowned with thorns; he had lost a great
> quantity of blood. So weakened he could
> scarcely walk, he yet had to carry this great load
> upon his shoulders. The soldiers struck him
> rudely, and he fell several times.

My Jesus, it is not the weight of the cross, but of my
sins, which has made you suffer so much pain. By the
merits of this first fall, deliver me from the misfortune
of falling into mortal sin.

I love you Jesus . . . Our Father. Hail Mary. Glory be.

FOURTH STATION

Jesus is met by his blessed mother

We adore . . .

> Consider the meeting of the Son and the mother, which took place on this journey. Their looks became like so many arrows to wound those hearts which loved each other so tenderly.

My sweet Jesus, by the sorrow you experienced in this meeting, grant me the grace of a truly devoted love for your most holy mother. And you, my queen, overwhelmed with sorrow, obtain for me, by your intercession a continual and tender remembrance of the passion of your Son.

I love you Jesus . . . Our Father. Hail Mary. Glory be.

FIFTH STATION

Simon of Cyrene helps Jesus to carry his cross

We adore . . .

> Consider how his cruel tormentors, seeing Jesus was on the point of expiring, and fearing he would die on the way, whereas they wished him to die the shameful death of the cross, constrained Simon of Cyrene to carry the cross behind our Lord.

My most beloved Jesus, I will not refuse the cross, as the Cyrenian did; I accept it, I embrace it. I accept in particular, the death you have destined for me, with all the pains which may accompany it; I unite it to your death; I offer it to you. You died for love of me; I will die for love of you. Help me by your grace.

I love you Jesus . . . Our Father. Hail Mary. Glory be.

SIXTH STATION

Veronica wipes the face of Jesus

We adore . . .

> Consider how the holy woman named
> Veronica, seeing Jesus so ill-used, and his face
> bathed in sweat and blood, presented him with
> a towel, with which he wiped his adorable face,
> leaving on it the impression of his holy
> countenance.

My most beloved Jesus, your face was beautiful before;
but in this journey it has lost all its beauty, and
wounds and blood have disfigured it. My soul also
was once beautiful, when it received your grace in
baptism; but I have disfigured it since by my sins. You
alone, my redeemer, by your passion, can restore it to
its former beauty.

I love you Jesus . . . Our Father. Hail Mary. Glory be.

SEVENTH STATION

Jesus falls the second time

We adore . . .

> Consider the second fall of Jesus under the
> cross; a fall which renews the pain of all the
> wounds in his head and members.

My most sweet Jesus, how many times have you
pardoned me, and how many times have I fallen
again, and begun again to offend you. By the merits of
this second fall, give me the necessary help to
persevere in your grace until death. Grant that in all
temptations which assail me, I may always commend
myself to you.

I love you Jesus . . . Our Father. Hail Mary. Glory be.

EIGHTH STATION

The women of Jerusalem mourn for our Lord

We adore . . .

> Consider how these women wept with
> compassion at seeing Jesus in such a pitiable
> state, streaming with blood, as he walked
> along. 'Daughters of Jerusalem,' said he, 'weep
> not for me, but for yourselves and for your
> children.'

My Jesus, laden with sorrows, I weep for the offences I
have committed against you, because of the pains they
have deserved, and still more because of the
displeasure they have caused you, who has loved me
so much. It is your love more than the fear of hell
which causes me to weep for my sins.

I love you Jesus . . . Our Father. Hail Mary. Glory be.

NINTH STATION

Jesus falls for the third time

We adore . . .

> Consider the third fall of Jesus Christ. His
> weakness was extreme, and the cruelty of his
> executioners excessive who tried to hasten his
> steps when he could scarcely move.

My outraged Jesus, by the merits of the weakness you
suffered in going to Calvary, give me strength
sufficient to conquer all human respect, and all my
wicked passions, which have led me to reject your
friendship.

I love you Jesus . . . Our Father. Hail Mary. Glory be.

TENTH STATION

Jesus is stripped of his garments

We adore . . .

Consider the violence with which Jesus was stripped by the executioners. His inner garments adhered to his torn flesh, and they dragged them off so roughly that the skin came with them. Take pity on your Saviour thus cruelly treated.

My innocent Jesus, by the merits of the torments you felt, help me to strip myself of all affection to things of earth, in order that I may place all my love in you, who are so worthy of my love.

I love you Jesus . . . Our Father. Hail Mary. Glory be.

ELEVENTH STATION

Jesus is nailed to the cross

We adore . . .

Consider how Jesus, having been placed upon the cross, extended his hands, and offered to his eternal Father the sacrifice of his life for our salvation. Those barbarians fastened him with nails, and then, securing the cross, allowed him to die with anguish on this infamous gibbet.

My Jesus, loaded with contempt, nail my heart to your feet, that it may ever remain there to love you and never quit you again.

I love you Jesus . . . Our Father. Hail Mary. Glory be.

TWELFTH STATION

Jesus dies on the cross

We adore . . .

> Consider how Jesus, being consumed with
> anguish after three hours' agony on the cross,
> abandoned himself to the weight of his body,
> bowed his head and died.

My dying Jesus, I kiss devoutly the cross on which you
died for love of me. I have merited by my sins to die a
miserable death. But your death is my hope. By the
merits of your death, give me grace to die embracing
your feet, and burning with love for you. I commit my
soul into your hands.

I love you Jesus . . . Our Father. Hail Mary. Glory be.

THIRTEENTH STATION

Jesus is taken down from the cross

We adore . . .

> Consider how, after our Lord had expired, two
> of his disciples, Joseph and Nicodemus, took
> him down from the cross and placed him in the
> arms of his afflicted mother, who received him
> with unutterable tenderness, and pressed him
> to her bosom.

Mother of sorrow, for the love of this Son, accept me
for your servant, and pray for me. And my redeemer,
since you have died for me, permit me to love you; for
I wish but you, and nothing more.

I love you Jesus . . . Our Father. Hail Mary. Glory be.

Jesus is placed in the tomb

We adore . . .

> Consider how the disciples carried the body of
> Jesus to bury it. Accompanied by his holy
> mother, who arranged it in the sepulchre with
> her own hands; they then closed the tomb, and
> all withdrew.

My buried Jesus, I kiss the stone that encloses you. But
you rose again the third day. I beseech you by your
resurrection, make me rise glorious with you at the last
day, to be always united with you in heaven to praise
you and love you for ever.

I love you Jesus . . . Our Father. Hail Mary. Glory be.

Let us Pray.
Lord Jesus Christ, you walked the way to Calvary to
rescue us from our sin, but the Father, pleased with
your obedient submission to his will, glorified you in
the resurrection. May we follow obediently in your
footsteps so that one day we may share in the glory of
your risen life. We make this prayer through you who
lives with the Father and Holy Spirit, one God for ever
and ever. **Amen.**

Devotion to the Five Sacred Wounds

Lord, Jesus Christ, we adore the sacred wound of your
left foot. We thank you for the pain which you
endured with so much love and charity. We suffer
with you in your sufferings, and we humbly beg
pardon for our sins, which we deplore beyond all else.
Convert all sinners, and make them understand the
enormity of rejecting your love.

Jesus, hear us.
Jesus, graciously hear us.

Lord Jesus Christ, we adore the sacred wound of your right foot. We thank you for the pain which you endured with so much love and charity. We suffer with you in your sufferings, and we pray that you would grant us strength against all temptations, and prompt obedience in the doing of your holy will. Comfort, O Jesus, the poor, the miserable, the afflicted, and all who are tempted or persecuted. Most just judge, govern those who administer justice, and assist all those who labour in the care of souls.
Jesus, hear us.
Jesus, graciously hear us.

Lord Jesus Christ, we adore the sacred wound of your left hand. We thank you for the pain which you endured with so much love and charity. We suffer with you in your sufferings, and we pray that you would give us the grace to earnestly desire heaven. Grant us patience in all the trials of this life, and conformity in all things to your blessed will. Pardon all our enemies, and all those who bear ill-will against us. Grant patience to the sick, and restore them to health; support with your grace all who are in their agony, that they may soon see your face in glory.
Jesus, hear us.
Jesus, graciously hear us.

Lord Jesus Christ, we adore the sacred wound in your right hand. We thank you for the pain which you endured with so much love and charity. We suffer with you in your sufferings, and we pray that you would grant us a resolute will to seek those things which are a help to our salvation. Grant us the grace of final perseverance, peace and relief to the souls in

purgatory, and daily lead nearer to true holiness your
servants in this world.
Jesus, hear us.
Jesus, graciously hear us.

Lord Jesus Christ, we adore the sacred wound in your
blessed side. We thank you for the infinite love
manifested towards us at the opening of your sacred
heart. Grant us a pure and perfect charity, that we may
love all things for your sake and you above all things,
and may we breathe our last in the presence of your
divine love. Protect your holy Catholic Church, direct
your vicar upon earth, bishops, priests and all who
labour for the sake of the gospel. Preserve in your holy
service all Christian kings and rulers. Bring back into
the way of salvation all those who have gone astray
and bring under your sacred will all the enemies of
your holy name.
Jesus, hear us.
Jesus, graciously hear us.

Let us pray.
Lord Jesus Christ, we honour the five wounds which
in your love you endured for us your servants whom
you have redeemed with your precious blood. Grant
that our devotion to them may console us with the
thought that one day, through the power of your
resurrection, we will be with you in paradise. We
make this prayer to the Father, who with you and the
Holy Spirit, lives and reigns God for ever and ever.
Amen.

Signs of sorrow and love
I kiss the wounds in your sacred head,
with sorrow deep and true,
may every thought of mine this day
be an act of love for you.

I kiss the wounds in your sacred hands,
with sorrow deep and true,
may every touch of my hands this day
be an act of love for you.

I kiss the wounds in your sacred feet,
with sorrow deep and true,
may every step I take this day
be an act of love for you.

I kiss the wound in your sacred side,
with sorrow deep and true,
may every beat of my heart this day
be an act of love for you.

Prayers to the Holy Spirit

The Holy Spirit is the gift of the risen Christ and his loving Father. Through him we pray to the Father and share in the fruits of the passion, death and resurrection of Jesus Christ. The Holy Spirit is the inspirer of all prayer. He is united with us in every thought, word and action which we offer to the Father so that the life of the risen Christ is always at work in us through his inspiration.

For the presence of the Holy Spirit

Come, Holy Spirit, fill the hearts of your faithful,
and enkindle in them the fire of your love.
Send forth your Spirit and they shall be created.
And you shall renew the face of the earth.
Let us pray.
O God, who has taught the hearts of the faithful by the light of the Holy Spirit, grant that by the gift of the same Spirit we may be always truly wise and ever rejoice in his consolation. **Amen.**

Come, Holy Ghost, creator, come
from thy bright heavenly throne,
come, take possession of our souls,
and make them all thine own.

Thou who art called the Paraclete,
best gift of God above,
the living spring, the living fire,
sweet unction and true love.

Thou who art sev'nfold in thy grace,
finger of God's right hand;
his promise, teaching little ones
to speak and understand.

O guide our minds with thy blest light,
with love our hearts inflame;
and with thy strength, which ne'er decays,
confirm our mortal flame.

Far from us drive our deadly foe;
true peace unto us bring;
and through all perils lead us safe
beneath thy sacred wing.

Through thee may we the Father know,
through thee th'eternal Son,
and thee the Spirit of them both,
thrice-blessed Three in One.

All glory to the Father be,
with his co-equal Son;
the same to thee, great Paraclete,
while endless ages run.

Ascribed to Rabanus Maurus.

Come down, O love divine,
seek thou this soul of mine,
and visit it with thine own
ardour glowing;
O comforter, draw near,
within my heart appear
and kindle it, thy holy
flame bestowing.

O let it freely burn,
till earthly passions turn

to dust and ashes in its
heat consuming;
and let thy glorious light
shine ever on my sight
and clothe me round, the while my
path illuming.

Let holy charity
mine outward vesture be,
and lowliness become mine
inner clothing;
true lowliness of heart,
which takes the humbler part,
and o'er its own shortcomings
weeps with loathing.

And so the yearning strong,
with which the soul will long,
shall far outpass the power of
human telling;
for none can guess its grace,
till he become the place
wherein the Holy Spirit
makes his dwelling.

Bianco da Siena.

O God, to whom all hearts are open, all hearts known,
and from whom no secrets are hidden, cleanse the
thoughts of our hearts by the inpouring of your Holy
Spirit, that every thought and word of ours may begin
from you, and in you be perfectly completed, through
Christ our Lord.

Holy Spirit come into our lives.
Open our ears   – to hear what you are saying to us
                  in the things that happen to us
                  in the people we meet.

Open our eyes   – to see the needs of the people round
                  us.
Open our hands – to do our work well
                  to help when help is needed.
Open our lips   – to tell others the good news of Jesus
                  and bring comfort, happiness and
                  laughter
                  to other people.
Open our minds – to discover new truth
                  about you and the world.
Open our hearts – to love you and our fellow men
                  as you have loved us in Jesus.
To you, with our Father and the Son, one God;
all honour and praise shall be given
now and for ever.

A prayer for awakening
Holy Spirit, come like a mighty rushing wind and
awaken us out of our complacency, our apathy, our
indifference. Disturb us, for we are too content to let
things go on as they are, and to let people go on not
knowing you. Penetrate the closed gates of our hearts
and make us live again. O Holy Spirit, create among us
a mighty Christian revolution and cast the fear of the
unknown out of our lives.

                            Michael Hollings and Etta Gullick*

Spirit of the living God,
      fall afresh on me.
Spirit of the living God,
      fall afresh on me.
Melt me, mould me,
      fill me, use me.
Spirit of the living God,
      fall afresh on me.

Spirit of the living God,
    fall afresh on us.
Spirit of the living God
    fall afresh on us.
Melt us, mould us,
    fill us, use us.
Spirit of the living God,
    fall afresh on us.

Michael Iverson

For the Gifts of the Holy Spirit

Spirit of wisdom, preside over all my thoughts, words
and actions,
from this hour till the moment of my death.
Spirit of understanding, enlighten and teach me.
Spirit of counsel, direct my experience.
Spirit of fortitude, strengthen my weakness.
Spirit of knowledge, instruct my ignorance.
Spirit of piety, make me fervent in good works.
Spirit of fear, restrain me from all evil.
Spirit of peace, give me your peace.
Heavenly Spirit, make me persevere in the service of
God the Father,
    and enable me to act on all occasions with
    goodness, patience, charity, joy, generosity,
    mildness and fidelity. Let the heavenly virtues of
    modesty, continence and chastity adorn the
    temple you have chosen for your abode, and, by
    your all-powerful grace, preserve my soul from
    the misfortune of sin.

Holy Spirit, as I awake and day begins
waken me to your presence;
waken me to your indwelling;

waken me to inward sight of you,
and speech with you
and strength from you;
that all my earthly walk may awaken into song
and my spirit leap up to you all day,
all ways.

Eric Milner-White*

Lord, no eye has seen, no ear has heard, no heart has conceived the things you have prepared for those who love you. Set us ablaze with the fire of the Holy Spirit, that we may love you in and above all things and so receive the rewards you have promised us through Christ our Lord.

A Christian's Prayer Book

Holy Spirit, make our lives new by your divine power, that we may live by the light of the resurrection and work in a manner inspired by you. May Christ, our brother, be with us today and every day, now and for ever.

Michael Buckley

Holy Spirit, I offer myself to your work of healing, peace and reconciliation. In my busy world bless my silent moments. In the stillness of my heart may I find peace within myself, peace with others and peace with you.

Michael Buckley

The Sacraments

*T*he Christian life is nourished by prayer and the sacraments. We celebrate in the sacraments the triumph of Christ over sin, death and the world. This he achieved through his passion, death and resurrection. The resurrection of Christ is the ultimate triumph in which the Christian shares through his oneness with the Lord. Since the resurrection our lives take on a new meaning. No sorrow is ultimate. Christ leads us through everything to final victory. We *celebrate* all the sacraments because we are an Easter people.

The relationship between God and us is personalised in Christ. God communicates to us through him. Conscious of being 'in Christ', the Church sees its sacramental ministry as the continuation of Christ's ministry. As Christ laid his hands on the sick, so does the Church. As he called the Holy Spirit to be his advocate for his followers, so does the Church. As he gave thanks and shared the bread and wine, so the Church represents and calls effectively into the present his sacrifice for our salvation.

The visible signs, or rites, of the sacraments effect and help us to be aware of our personal encounter with Christ. He sanctifies every aspect of our lives, which he presents to our loving Father. Christ meets us in the sacraments at the points of our spiritual growth.

The Christian life, like all life, has a beginning. This is called 'initiation'. The whole process of initiation marks the beginning of our Christian pilgrimage, which finds its completion in the kingdom of heaven. There, there will be no need of sacraments because then we will see God 'face to face'.

The sacraments of initiation are baptism, confirmation and eucharist.

Baptism incorporates us into the body of Christ, the Church and is the sacrament of new life.
Confirmation, which gives us the fullness of the Holy Spirit, is inseparably linked to baptism and is its completion.
The Eucharist, which makes the sacrifice of Christ present and active among us, is the central sacrament in the life of the Church.

There are four other sacraments which help us on our Christian pilgrimage to God, our Father.
Reconciliation is the sacrament which reconciles us to God, whose love we have forsaken through personal sin.
Marriage sanctifies the daily life of husband and wife, and their children.
Holy Orders perpetuates the special ministry of Christ in his Church.

Anointing of the Sick ensures Christ's saving help for us in times of sickness.

From birth to death Christ's resurrection is at work in us. The sacraments are the activity of Christ in our midst, offering praise to the Father, and reconciling us to God and to one another.

Baptism

Baptism is an Easter sacrament. Through it we are made one with the risen Lord and enter into his risen life. When we were baptised we went into the tomb with him and joined him in death, so that as Christ was raised from the dead by the Father's glory, we too might live a new life. *Romans 6:4. Our 'new life' means that we are God's own children in whom Christ's Spirit dwells in a special way. We dare to call God 'Abba', Father, for that is what he is to us in this new relationship. We leave spiritual death behind us for the new life of grace.*

Renewal of Baptismal Vows

Today I freely acknowledge my commitment to Christ, through my baptismal vows which I renew as a sign and pledge of my Christian faith. I therefore, reject Satan and all his works and empty promises. I believe in God, the Father almighty, creator of heaven and earth. I believe in Jesus Christ, his only Son our Lord, who was born of the Virgin Mary, was crucified, died, and was buried, rose from the dead, and is now seated at the right hand of the Father. I believe in the Holy Spirit, the holy Catholic Church, the communion of saints, the resurrection of the body, and life everlasting. This is my faith. This is the faith of the Church. I am proud to profess it, in Christ Jesus our Lord. Amen.

or

All powerful and merciful God, Father of our Lord Jesus Christ, who freed me from sin and spiritual death, and gave me the new life of grace through water and the Holy Spirit, I renew my baptismal vows and rededicate my life to your loving protection so that, day by day, I may grow in your knowledge, love and service, through Christ our Lord. Amen.

Prayers for parents, godparents and all baptised

For the baptised person
Heavenly Father, we pray that this child, true to his/her baptismal vows, may walk in the light of the resurrection and be true to the gospel of your Son so that one day he/she may see you with unveiled face. Amen.

For the mother
God the Father, through his Son, the Virgin Mary's child, has brought joy to all Christian mothers, as they see the hope of eternal life shine on their children. May he bless the mother of this child. She now thanks God for the gift of her child. May she be one with him (her) in thanking God for ever in heaven, in Christ Jesus our Lord. Amen.

For the father
God, is the giver of all life, human and divine. May he bless the father of this child. He and his wife will be the first teachers of their child in the ways of faith. May they be also the best of teachers, bearing witness to the faith by what they say and do, in Christ Jesus our Lord. Amen.

For godparents
Heavenly Father, may the godparents of this child be so inspired by the Holy Spirit that they may always be sensitive to the power of the gospel at work in the life

of their godchild. May they lead him/her by word
and example to a true following of Jesus Christ, your
only Son our Lord. Amen.

Michael Buckley

By godparents

Bless us, Lord, that we may fulfil the Christian task
entrusted to us. May the example of our lives help our
godchild to come to a deeper understanding of the
Christian faith and so grow in age and wisdom before
God and men. Bless our godchild that he/she may be
faithful to his/her baptismal vows and together, as we
witness to the gospel, may we all one day behold your
sacred countenance. We make this prayer through
Christ our Lord. Amen.

Michael Buckley

For all baptised Christians

By God's gift, through water and the Holy Spirit, we
are reborn to everlasting life. In his goodness, may he
continue to pour out his blessings upon all his sons
and daughters. May he make them always, wherever
they may be, faithful members of his holy people and
may he send his peace upon all, in Christ Jesus our
Lord. Amen.

Michael Buckley

For cathechumens

May their preparation, to receive the sacrament of
baptism, be not merely in their understanding of the
teaching of the Church, but also in the conduct of their
daily lives. Day by day may they be made more
ready to be baptised into the body of the risen Lord;
share the gifts of the Holy Spirit, and become children
of the Father.

By cathechumens

Eternal Father, who created us and made us members of the human family, be with us in our preparation to acknowledge Jesus as Lord of our lives. In all that we say and do, may we be made ready to receive the sacrament which gives us a fuller sharing in gifts of the Holy Spirit and enables us to share at the table of the Lord in the fellowship of his Church.

For those preparing for confirmation

Father, may those who have already been baptised by water and the Holy Spirit persevere faithfully in their Christian vocation. May they fervently receive the sacrament of confirmation, by which they will be given the spirit of wisdom and understanding, the spirit of right judgment and courage, the spirit of knowledge and reverence and so live the full life of Christians, totally committed to the service of your kingdom.

For the confirmed

God, our Father, complete the work you have begun and keep the gifts of your Holy Spirit active in the hearts of those who have been confirmed. Make them ready to live his gospel and eager to do his will. May they never be ashamed to proclaim to all the world Christ crucified, living and reigning for ever and ever. Amen.

Eucharist: Sacrament and Sacrifice

The eucharist is the centre of our relationship with God the Father, Son and Holy Spirit. It unites us on earth as a community committed to Christ and to one another. As Christians, we are, above all else, a eucharistic community.

'The eucharist makes the Church' because it is the centre towards which all other sacraments are orientated, and the source from which they derive their power. All the sacraments are ideally celebrated within the context of the eucharist. The eucharist is, *par excellence*, the sacred action by which God gives himself to us, and through which we give glory to him through our brother and Lord, Jesus the Christ. It is a reciprocal flow so that God's gift to us in Christ is at the same time our response to him.

The eucharist is both a sacrifice and a sacrament since the one essentially involves the other. The victim (sacrifice), Christ, is the meal (sacrament). The eucharist is a sacrifice which is identified with Calvary. Christ is our paschal lamb who sacrificed himself for us on the cross so that by his body and blood we are nourished as the new people of God.

When we celebrate the eucharist we call effectively into our lives the presence of Christ's body and blood, soul and divinity, which alone reconciles us to the Father. In it we celebrate, at Christ's command, the memory of what he did for us. We thank him for what he has done and in joyful anticipation we celebrate the eucharist until he comes again in glory.

The eucharist is also a sacrament. Saint Paul compares the Church to the body of Christ of which we are all members. The food for that body is the eucharist so that holy communion makes us a community: *The blessing-cup that we bless is a communion with the blood of Christ, and the bread that we break is a communion with the body of Christ. The fact that there is only one loaf means that, though there are many of us, we form a single body because we all have a share in this one loaf* 1 Corinthians 10:16–17.

In the eucharist we share with God and one another in a unique way. The eucharist is for sanctification and mission. It unites us to God, and sends us forth to proclaim to the world the saving power of the Lord Jesus Christ. The eucharist, the third and final sacrament of initiation, is our pledge of future glory and we approach the altar remembering the Lord's promise: *Anyone who does eat my flesh and drink my blood has eternal life, and I shall raise him up on the last day. For my flesh is real food and my blood is real drink. He who eats my flesh and drinks my blood lives in me and I live in him.* John 6:54–56. The eucharist is a share not only in Christ's death but also in his resurrection.

The Sacrifice: the Mass

*The Mass is the effective commemoration of what Christ did
for us on the cross. By the power of his Spirit he re-presents
this sacrifice on our altars, so that honour, praise, adoration
and thanksgiving may be continually given to the Father.
The Mass is filled with joy and hope because in it we celebrate
the Lord's death and resurrection until he comes again. In
one action it telescopes all time, past, present, and future:*
Christ has died, Christ is risen, Christ will come again.

Prayers before Mass

To the Holy Trinity

Receive, most Holy Trinity, this holy sacrifice of the
body and blood of our Lord Jesus Christ which, by the
hands of your priest, I, your unworthy servant, now
offer to your divine majesty. I unite it with all the
masses which have ever been or will be offered to you,
in union with the sacrifice of Christ our Lord on the
cross, and according to his will and that of his holy
Church. Through it may I share in the resurrection of
your Son who in rising from the dead is our sure hope
of eternal salvation.

For the sanctification of Sunday

Almighty and eternal God, who has appointed six
days in which we may labour, and has consecrated the
seventh to yourself, grant that we may sanctify this
day as you have commanded by devoting it to your
service. Mercifully forgive us all our past neglect,
pardon the sins of which we have been guilty during

the week, and give us the grace to avoid them for the future.

An offering prayer

Most merciful Father, you so loved the world that you sent your only Son on earth to redeem and save us. In obedience to your will he humbled himself, even to death on a cross. He continues to offer himself daily through the ministry of his priests for the living and the dead. We humbly pray that, motivated by a living faith, we may always assist with devotion and reverence at the oblation of his most precious body and blood which is made at Mass. In this way, we share in the supreme sacrifice which he accomplished on Calvary; and his resurrection from the dead.
In union with the whole Church, and in the company of the Blessed Virgin Mary and all the angels and saints, we now offer the adorable sacrifice of the Mass to your honour and glory. In it we acknowledge your infinite perfections, your supreme dominion over all creatures, our entire submission to you and our dependence on your gracious providence. We offer it in thanksgiving for your goodness to us and for the forgiveness of our sins.
We offer it also for the spread of the Catholic Church throughout the world and for our Pope, bishop and all the pastors that they may direct the faithful in the way of salvation. In this Mass we pray for peace and goodwill among all peoples and for the needs of our world. May we, here present, receive grace to live a Christian life in this world in order to be with you in the world to come. We offer it for the eternal repose of the faithful departed.
In this Mass we remember, with gratitude, all that your Son Jesus Christ suffered for love of us as we commemorate his bitter passion and death, his

glorious resurrection and ascension into heaven. We offer it for all the intentions agreeable to your holy will through the same Jesus Christ, your Son, our Lord who is both priest and victim. We make our prayer in the name of the most Holy Trinity, Father, Son and Holy Spirit to whom be honour, praise and glory for ever and ever. Amen.

To God, the Father
Eternal Father, I offer you all the masses celebrated this day throughout the world for sinners in their agony, and for those who shall be overtaken by death today. May they obtain mercy through the precious blood of Jesus their redeemer, and may the same precious blood obtain satisfaction for my sins and a share in the resurrection of your Son. Amen.

To God, the Son
Lord Jesus Christ, to whom belongs all that is in heaven and earth, I desire to consecrate myself wholly to you and to be yours for evermore. This day I offer myself to you in singleness of heart, to serve and obey you always, and I offer you without ceasing, a sacrifice of praise and thanksgiving. Receive me, O my Saviour, in union with the holy oblation of your precious blood which I offer to you this day, in the presence of angels, that this sacrifice may avail unto my salvation and that of the whole world.

Thomas à Kempis

At the Lamb's high feast we sing
praise to our victorious king,
who hath washed us in the tide
flowing from his pierced side.
Praise we him whose love divine
gives the guests his blood for wine,

gives his body for the feast,
love the victim, love the priest.

Where the paschal blood is poured,
Death's dark angel sheathes his sword;
Israel's hosts triumphant go
through the wave that drowns the foe.
Christ the Lamb, whose blood was shed.
Paschal victim, paschal bread;
with sincerity and love
eat we manna from above.

Mighty victim from the sky,
powers of hell beneath thee lie;
death is conquered in the fight;
thou hast brought us life and light,
now thy banner thou dost wave;
vanquished Satan and the grave;
angels join his praise to tell –
see o'erthrown the prince of hell.

Paschal triumph, paschal joy,
only sin can this destroy;
from the death of sin set free
souls re-born, dear Lord, in thee.
Hymns of glory, songs of praise,
Father, unto thee we raise.
Risen Lord, all praise to thee,
ever with the Spirit be.

7th-century, translation Robert Campbell

To God the Holy Spirit

Holy Spirit, cleanse our minds and hearts so that we may celebrate with joy the mysteries of our redemption in this holy Mass. Be near us as we bring our gifts to the Father, in union with the Son, who as our supreme high priest has gone through to the highest heaven there to make intercession for us. Fill us with confidence in approaching the throne of grace where, with all the angels and saints, we shall render due homage through Jesus Christ who with you and the Father lives and reigns, God, for ever and ever. Amen.

To Our Lady

Mother of mercy and love, blessed Virgin Mary, I turn to you in confidence. You stood by your Son as he hung dying on the cross. Stand also by me and by all those who assist at Mass today, here and throughout the entire Church. Help us to offer a perfect and acceptable sacrifice in the sight of the holy and undivided Trinity, our most high God.

To Saint Joseph

God, our Father, just as you allowed Joseph to touch with his hands, and bear in his arms your only Son, Jesus Christ, so also may we, through cleanness of heart and blamelessness of life, be worthy to assist at Mass and thus may we be better prepared for the banquet of the kingdom.

To our guardian angel and all the saints

May my guardian angel, and all the saints especially my patron Saint N., intercede for me that I may be worthy to assist in offering this sacrifice to almighty God, for the praise and glory of his name, for our good, and the good of all his Church.

The saint of the day

Saint N., in whose honour the holy sacrifice of the body and blood is this day offered to God the Father, intercede for me with the Holy Spirit that I be given the grace to participate in this great sacrifice in a worthy and acceptable manner, and so with you and all the saints come to sing the praises of God eternally in our heavenly home.

Excerpts from the Psalms
I rejoiced when I heard them say:
'Let us go to God's house.'
And now our feet are standing
within your gates, O Jerusalem.
For love of my brethren and friends
I say: 'Peace upon you!'
For love of the house of the Lord
I will ask for your good.

Psalm 121

Cry out with joy to the Lord, all the earth.
Serve the Lord with gladness.
Come before him singing for joy.
Go within his gates, giving thanks.
Enter his courts with songs of praise,
Give thanks to him and bless his name.

Psalm 99

How lovely is your dwelling place,
Lord, God of hosts.
My soul is longing and yearning,
is yearning for the courts of the Lord.
They are happy, who dwell in your house,
for ever singing your praise.
One day within your courts
is better than a thousand elsewhere.

Psalm 83

The order of Mass

Introductory Rites

ENTRANCE PROCESSION

All stand
The entrance song fits the theme of the season and occasion. If there is no singing then all say the entrance antiphon.

Entrance song or antiphon: *Proper of the Day*

In the name of the Father, and of the Son, and of the Holy Spirit.
Amen.

GREETING
The priest greets the people in one of the following ways:

1. The grace of our Lord Jesus Christ and the love of God
and the fellowship of the Holy Spirit be with you all.
And also with you.
or
2. The grace and peace of God our Father and the Lord Jesus Christ be with you.
Blessed be God, the Father of our Lord Jesus Christ.
or
And also with you.
3. The Lord be with you.
And also with you.

THEME OF THE MASS
The priest may introduce the theme of the Mass.

PENITENTIAL RITE OR RITE OF SPRINKLING
The rite of sprinkling may be celebrated instead of the penitential rite.

PENITENTIAL RITE

The priest invites us to recall our sins, and repent of them in silence, in these or similar words:

My brothers and sisters,
to prepare ourselves to celebrate the sacred mysteries,
let us call to mind our sins.

After a brief silence one of the following three forms is used.

1.   **I confess to almighty God,**
     and to you, my brothers and sisters,
     that I have sinned through my own fault
     All strike their breast

     in my thoughts and in my words,
     in what I have done,
     and in what I have failed to do;
     and I ask blessed Mary, ever virgin,
     all the angels and saints,
     and you, my brothers and sisters,
     to pray for me to the Lord our God.

2.   Lord, we have sinned against you:
Lord, have mercy.
     Lord, have mercy.
Lord, show us your mercy and love.
     And grant us your salvation.
          or

3.   You were sent to heal the contrite:
Lord, have mercy.
     Lord, have mercy.
You came to call sinners:
Christ, have mercy.
     Christ, have mercy.
You plead for us at the right hand of the Father:
Lord, have mercy.
     Lord, have mercy.

The third form may also use similar invocations but the people's response always remains the same.
May almighty God have mercy on us,
forgive us our sins,
and bring us to everlasting life.
Amen.

RITE OF BLESSING AND SPRINKLING OF HOLY WATER
When this rite is celebrated it replaces the penitential rite. The Kyrie is also omitted.
The priest blesses the water using these or similar words:
Dear friends,
 this water will be used
 to remind us of our baptism.
 Let us ask God to bless it
 and to keep us faithful
 to the Spirit he has given us.
God our Father,
 your gift of water
 brings life and freshness to the earth;
 it washes away our sins
 and brings us eternal life.
We ask you now
 to bless † this water,
 and to give us your protection on this day
 which you have made your own.
 Renew the living spring of your life within us
 and protect us in spirit and body,
 that we may be free from sin
 and come into your presence
 to receive your gift of salvation.

During the Easter season.
Lord God almighty,
 hear the prayers of your people:
 we celebrate our creation and redemption.

Hear our prayers and bless ✝ this water
which gives fruitfulness to the fields,
and refreshment and cleansing to man.
You chose water to show your goodness
when you led your people to freedom
through the Red Sea
and satisfied their thirst in the desert
with water from the rock.
Water was the symbol used by the prophets
to foretell your new covenant with man.
You made the water of baptism holy
by Christ's baptism in the Jordan:
by it you gave us a new birth
and renew us in holiness.
May this water remind us of our baptism,
and let us share the joy
of all who have been baptised at Easter.

*Where necessary, salt is blessed and mixed with the holy
water. After the sprinkling, the rite is concluded with the
following prayer.*

May almighty God cleanse us of our sins,
and through the eucharist we celebrate
make us worthy to sit at his table
in his heavenly kingdom.
Amen.

THE KYRIE
If this has already been used in form three of the
penitential rite or when the blessing and sprinkling of
holy water takes place it is not said here.
Lord have mercy.
Lord, have mercy
Christ, have mercy.
Christ, have mercy.

Lord, have mercy.
Lord, have mercy.

THE GLORIA
This triumphant hymn of praise is sung or said on
Sundays outside of the seasons of Advent and Lent,
on solemnities and feasts, and on some other
occasions of special importance.

> **Glory to God in the highest,**
> > **and peace to his people on earth.**
> **Lord God, heavenly King,**
> **almighty God and Father,**
> > **we worship you, we give you thanks,**
> > **we praise you for your glory.**
> **Lord Jesus Christ, only Son of the Father,**
> **Lord God, Lamb of God,**
> **you take away the sin of the world:**
> > **have mercy on us;**
> **you are seated at the right hand of the Father**
> > **receive our prayer.**
> **For you alone are the Holy One,**
> **you alone are the Lord,**
> **you alone are the Most High,**
> > **Jesus Christ,**
> > **with the Holy Spirit,**
> > **in the glory of God the Father. Amen.**

OPENING PRAYER: *Proper of the Day*

After an invitation to prayer, priest and people pray
silently for a while. At the end of the opening prayer
said by the priest, the people respond:
Amen.

Liturgy of the Word

FIRST READING
All sit
At the end of the reading:
Reader: This is the Word of the Lord.
Thanks be to God.

RESPONSORIAL PSALM
The cantor (reader) sings or recites the psalm to which the people make the response.

SECOND READING
At the end of the reading:
Reader: This is the Word of the Lord.
Thanks be to God.

PROCLAMATION OF THE GOSPEL
All stand

ALLELUIA OR GOSPEL ACCLAMATION:
Proper of the Day

The Lord be with you.
and also with you.
A reading from the holy gospel according to N.
Glory to you, Lord.
At the end of the gospel the priest or deacon says:
This is the gospel of the Lord.
Praise to you, Lord Jesus Christ.

HOMILY
All sit

PROFESSION OF FAITH
All stand
We believe in one God,
    the Father, the Almighty,
    maker of heaven and earth,
    of all that is seen and unseen.

We believe in one Lord, Jesus Christ,
the only Son of God,
eternally begotten of the Father,
God from God, Light from Light,
true God from true God,
begotten, not made,
one in Being with the Father.
Through him all things were made.
For us men and for our salvation
he came down from heaven: *All bow*
by the power of the Holy Spirit
he was born of the Virgin Mary,
and became man.
For our sake he was crucified under Pontius
Pilate;
he suffered, died, and was buried.
On the third day he rose again
in fulfillment of the Scriptures;
he ascended into heaven
and is seated at the right hand of the
Father.
He will come again in glory to judge the living
and the dead,
and his kingdom will have no end.
We believe in the Holy Spirit, the Lord, the giver of
life,
who proceeds from the Father and the Son.
With the Father and the Son he is worshiped
and glorified.
he has spoken through the prophets.
We believe in one holy catholic and apostolic
Church.
We acknowledge one baptism for the forgiveness
of sins.

**We look for the resurrection of the dead,
and the life of the world to come. Amen.**

PRAYER OF THE FAITHFUL
The people respond to each intercession with the
appropriate response. Finally, the priest says the
concluding prayer to which the people respond:
Amen.

Liturgy of the Eucharist

Preparation of the Altar and Gifts

PROCESSION WITH GIFTS
If no hymn is sung during the procession then the
people join in by making their responses to the prayers
of offering:

Blessed are you, Lord, God of all creation.
Through your goodness we have this bread to offer,
which earth has given and human hands have made.
It will become for us the bread of life.
Blessed be God for ever.
By the mystery of this water and wine may we come to
share in the divinity of Christ, who humbled himself to
share in our humanity.
Blessed are you, Lord, God of all creation.
Through your goodness we have this wine to offer,
fruit of the vine and work of human hands.
It will become our spiritual drink.
Blessed be God for ever.
Lord God we ask you to receive us and be pleased with
the sacrifice we offer you with humble and contrite
hearts.

PRAYER OVER THE GIFTS
All stand

Pray, brethren, that our sacrifice
may be acceptable to God, the almighty Father.

> **May the Lord accept the sacrifice at your hands
> for the praise and glory of his name,
> for our good, and the good of all his Church.**

Prayer over the Gifts: *Proper of the Day*
At the end of the prayer the people respond: **Amen.**

The Eucharistic Prayer
All kneel

INTRODUCTORY DIALOGUE
The Lord be with you.
> **And also with you.**

Lift up your hearts.
> **We lift them up to the Lord.**

Let us give thanks to the Lord our God.
> **It is right to give him thanks and praise.**

THE PREFACE
At the end of the Preface all sing or say aloud:

> **Holy, holy, holy Lord, God of power and might,
> heaven and earth are full of your glory.**
> > **Hosanna in the highest.**
> **Blessed is he who comes in the name of the Lord.**
> > **Hosanna in the highest.**

There are many ways of thanking God for all he has
accomplished for us through Christ.
> Eucharistic Prayer I see page 76.
> Eucharistic Prayer II see page 80.
> Eucharistic Prayer III see page 83.
> Eucharistic Prayer IV see page 87.

Eucharistic Prayer I

The passages within the brackets may be omitted if the celebrant wishes.

We come to you, Father,
with praise and thanksgiving,
through Jesus Christ your Son.
Through him we ask you to accept and bless†
these gifts we offer you in sacrifice.

We pray for the Church

We offer them for your holy Catholic Church,
watch over it, Lord, and guide it;
grant it peace and unity throughout the world.
We offer them for N. our Pope,
for N. our bishop,
and for all who hold and teach the Catholic faith
that comes to us from the apostles.

For the living

Remember, Lord, your people,
especially those for whom we now pray, N. and N.
Remember all of us gathered here before you.
You know how firmly we believe in you
and dedicate ourselves to you.
We offer you this sacrifice of praise
for ourselves and those who are dear to us.
We pray to you, our living and true God,
for our well-being and redemption.

To honour the saints

In union with the whole Church
we honour Mary,
the ever-virgin mother of Jesus Christ our Lord and
    God,
We honour Joseph, her husband,
the apostles and martyrs
Peter and Paul, Andrew,

(James, John, Thomas,
James, Philip,
Bartholomew, Matthew, Simon and Jude;
we honour Linus, Cletus, Clement, Sixtus,
Cornelius, Cyprian, Lawrence, Chrysogonus,
John and Paul, Cosmas and Damian)
and all the saints.
May their merits and prayers
gain us your constant help and protection.
(Through Christ our Lord. Amen.)

For acceptance of this offering
Father, accept this offering
from your whole family.
Grant us your peace in this life,
save us from final damnation,
and count us among those you have chosen.
(Through Christ our Lord. Amen.)
Bless and approve our offering;
make it acceptable to you,
an offering in spirit and in truth.
Let it become for us
the body and blood of Jesus Christ,
your only Son, our Lord.
(Through Christ our Lord. Amen.)

The Lord's supper: the consecration
The day before he suffered
he took bread in his sacred hands
and looking up to heaven,
to you, his almighty Father,
he gave you thanks and praise.
He broke the bread,
gave it to his disciples, and said:

Take this, all of you, and eat it:
this is my body which will be given up for you.

When supper was ended,
he took the cup.
Again he gave you thanks and praise,
gave the cup to his disciples, and said:
Take this, all of you, and drink from it:
this is the cup of my blood,
the blood of the new and everlasting covenant.
It will be shed for you and for all
so that sins may be forgiven.
Do this in memory of me.

Memorial acclamation of the people
Let us proclaim the mystery of faith:
1. **Christ has died,**
   Christ is risen,
   Christ will come again.
2. **Dying you destroyed our death,**
   rising you restored our life.
   Lord Jesus, come in glory.
3. **When we eat this bread and drink this cup,**
   we proclaim your death, Lord Jesus,
   until you come in glory.
4. **Lord, by your cross and resurrection**
   you have set us free.
   You are the Saviour of the world.

Memorial of the paschal mystery and offering.
Father, we celebrate the memory of Christ, your Son.
We, your people and your ministers,
recall his passion,
his resurrection from the dead,
and his ascension into glory;
and from the many gifts you have given us
we offer to you, God of glory and majesty,
this holy and perfect sacrifice:

the bread of life
and the cup of eternal salvation.

Look with favour on these offerings
and accept them as once you accepted
the gifts of your servant Abel,
the sacrifice of Abraham, our father in faith,
and the bread and wine offered by your priest
Melchisedech.

Almighty God,
we pray that your angel may take this sacrifice
to your altar in heaven.
Then, as we receive from this altar
the sacred body and blood of your Son,
let us be filled with every grace and blessing.
(Through Christ our Lord. Amen.)

For the dead
Remember, Lord, those who have died
and have gone before us marked with the sign of faith,
especially those for whom we now pray, N. and N.
May these, and all who sleep in Christ,
find in your presence
light, happiness, and peace.
(Through Christ our Lord. Amen.)

For us sinners
For ourselves, too, we ask
some share in the fellowship of your apostles and martyrs,
with John the Baptist, Stephen, Matthias, Barnabas,
(Ignatius, Alexander, Marcellinus, Peter,
Felicity, Perpetua, Agatha, Lucy,
Agnes, Cecilia, Anastasia)
and all the saints.
Though we are sinners,
we trust in your mercy and love.

Do not consider what we truly deserve,
but grant us your forgiveness.
Through him
you give us all these gifts.
You fill them with life and goodness,
you bless them and make them holy.

Final doxology: in praise of God
Through him,
with him,
in him,
in the unity of the Holy Spirit,
all glory and honour is yours,
almighty Father,
for ever and ever.
   Amen.
[Turn to page 91.]

Eucharistic Prayer II

Preface (This may be replaced by another preface.)
Father, it is our duty and our salvation,
always and everywhere
to give you thanks
through your beloved Son, Jesus Christ.
He is the Word through whom you made the universe,
the Saviour you sent to redeem us.
By the power of the Holy Spirit
he took flesh and was born of the Virgin Mary.
For our sake he opened his arms on the cross;
he put an end to death
and revealed the resurrection.
In this he fulfilled your will
and won for you a holy people.
And so we join the angels and the saints
in proclaiming your glory
as we sing (say):

**Holy, holy, holy Lord, God of power and might,
heaven and earth are full of your glory.
Hosanna in the highest.
Blessed is he who comes in the name of the Lord.
Hosanna in the highest.**

Invocation of the Holy Spirit
Lord, you are holy indeed,
the fountain of all holiness.
Let your Spirit come upon these gifts to make them
holy,
so that they may become for us
the body and blood of our Lord, Jesus Christ.

The Lord's Supper
Before he was given up to death,
a death he freely accepted,
he took bread and gave you thanks.
He broke the bread,
gave it to his disciples, and said:
Take this, all of you, and eat it:
this is my body which will be given up for you.

When supper was ended, he took the cup.
Again he gave you thanks and praise,
gave the cup to his disciples, and said:
Take this, all of you, and drink from it:
this is the cup of my blood,
the blood of the new and everlasting covenant.
It will be shed for you and for all
so that sins may be forgiven.
Do this in memory of me.

Memorial acclamation of the people
Let us proclaim the mystery of faith:
1. **Christ has died,
   Christ is risen,
   Christ will come again.**

2. **Dying you destroyed our death,**
   rising you restored our life.
   Lord Jesus, come in glory.
3. **When we eat this bread and drink this cup,**
   we proclaim your death, Lord Jesus,
   until you come in glory.
4. **Lord, by your cross and resurrection**
   you have set us free.
   You are the Saviour of the world.

The memorial prayer
In memory of his death and resurrection,
we offer you, Father, this life-giving bread,
this saving cup.
We thank you for counting us worthy
to stand in your presence and serve you.
May all of us who share in the body and blood of
     Christ
be brought together in unity by the Holy Spirit.

Intercessions for the Church
Lord, remember your Church throughout the world;
make us grow in love,
together with N. our Pope,
N. our bishop, and all the clergy.

For the dead
(In masses for the dead the following may be added:)
Remember N. whom you have called from this life.
In baptism he (she) died with Christ:
may he (she) also share his resurrection.
Remember our brothers and sisters
who have gone to their rest
in the hope of rising again;
bring them and all the departed
into the light of your presence.

Have mercy on us all;
make us worthy to share eternal life
with Mary, the virgin Mother of God,
with the apostles, and with all the saints
who have done your will throughout the ages.
May we praise you in union with them,
and give you glory
through your Son, Jesus Christ.

Final doxology: in praise of God
Through him,
with him,
in him,
in the unity of the Holy Spirit,
all glory and honour is yours,
almighty Father,
for ever and ever.
> **Amen.**

[Turn to page 91.]

Eucharistic Prayer III

Praise to the Father
Father, you are holy indeed,
and all creation rightly gives you praise.
All life, all holiness comes from you
through your Son, Jesus Christ our Lord,
by the working of the Holy Spirit.
From age to age you gather a people to yourself,
so that from east to west
a perfect offering may be made
to the glory of your name.

Invocation of the Holy Spirit
And so, Father, we bring you these gifts.

We ask you to make them holy by the power of your
    Spirit,
that they may become the body and blood
of your Son, our Lord Jesus Christ,
at whose command we celebrate this eucharist.

The Lord's Supper
On the night he was betrayed,
he took bread and gave you thanks and praise.
He broke the bread, gave it to his disciples, and said:
Take this, all of you, and eat it:
this is my body which will be given up for you.

When supper was ended, he took the cup.
Again he gave you thanks and praise,
gave the cup to his disciples, and said:

Take this, all of you, and drink from it:
this is the cup of my blood,
the blood of the new and everlasting covenant.
It will be shed for you and for all
so that sins may be forgiven.
Do this in memory of me.

Memorial acclamation of the people
Let us proclaim the mystery of faith:
1. **Christ has died,**
   Christ is risen,
   Christ will come again.
2. **Dying you destroyed our death,**
   rising you restored our life.
   Lord Jesus, come in glory.
3. **When we eat this bread and drink this cup,**
   we proclaim your death, Lord Jesus,
   until you come in glory.
4. **Lord, by your cross and resurrection**
   you have set us free.
   You are the Saviour of the world.

84

The memorial prayer

Father, calling to mind the death your Son endured
for our salvation,
his glorious resurrection and ascension into heaven,
and ready to greet him when he comes again,
we offer you in thanksgiving this holy and living
sacrifice.
Look with favour on your Church's offering.
and see the Victim whose death has reconciled us to
yourself.
Grant that we, who are nourished by his body and
blood,
may be filled with his Holy Spirit,
and become one body, one spirit in Christ.

In communion with the saints

May he make us an everlasting gift to you
and enable us to share in the inheritance of your
saints,
with Mary, the virgin Mother of God;
with the apostles, the martyrs,
(Saint N. the saint of the day or patron saint) and all
your saints,
on whose constant intercession we rely for help.

Intercessions for the Church

Lord, may this sacrifice,
which has made our peace with you,
advance the peace and salvation of all the world.
Strengthen in faith and love your pilgrim Church on
earth;
your servant, Pope N., our bishop N.,
and all the bishops,

with the clergy and the entire people your Son has
gained for you.
Father, hear the prayers of the family you have
gathered here before you.
In mercy and love unite all your children wherever
they may be.

For the dead
Welcome into your kingdom our departed brothers
and sisters,
and all who have left this world in your friendship.
We hope to enjoy for ever the vision of your glory,
through Christ our Lord, from whom all good things
come.

(When this eucharistic prayer is used in masses for the
dead, the following may be said:)
Remember *N.*,
In baptism he (she) died with Christ:
may he (she) also share his resurrection,
when Christ will raise our mortal bodies
and make them like his own in glory.
Welcome into your kingdom our departed brothers
and sisters,
and all who have left this world in your friendship.
There we hope to share in your glory
when every tear will be wiped away.
On that day we shall see you, our God, as you are.
We shall become like you
and praise you for ever through Christ our Lord,
from whom all good things come.

Final doxology: in praise of God
Through him,
with him,
in him,
in the unity of the Holy Spirit,

all glory and honour is yours,
almighty Father,
for ever and ever.

Amen.
[Turn to page 91.]

Eucharistic Prayer IV

Preface
Father in heaven,
it is right that we should give you thanks and glory:
you are the one God, living and true.
Through all eternity you live in unapproachable light.
Source of life and goodness, you have created all
    things,
to fill your creatures with every blessing
and lead all men to the joyful vision of your light.
Countless hosts of angels stand before you to do your
    will;
they look upon your splendour
and praise you, night and day.
United with them,
and in the name of every creature under heaven,
we too praise your glory as we sing (say):
**Holy, holy, holy Lord, God of power and might,
heaven and earth are full of your glory.
    Hosanna in the highest.
Blessed is he who comes in the name of the Lord.
    Hosanna in the highest.**

Praise to the Father
Father, we acknowledge your greatness:
all your actions show your wisdom and love.
You formed man in your own likeness:
and set him over the whole world
to serve you, his creator,

and to rule over all creatures.
Even when he disobeyed you and lost your friendship
you did not abandon him to the power of death,
but helped all men to seek and find you.
Again and again you offered to man a covenant,
and through the prophets taught him to hope for
    salvation.
Father, you so loved the world
that in the fullness of time you sent your only Son to be
    our Saviour.
He was conceived through the power of the Holy
Spirit,
and born of the Virgin Mary,
a man like us in all things but sin.
To the poor he proclaimed the good news of
salvation,
to prisoners, freedom,
and to those in sorrow, joy.
In fulfilment of your will
he gave himself up to death;
but by rising from the dead,
he destroyed death and restored life.
And that we might live no longer for ourselves but for
    him,
he sent the Holy Spirit from you, Father,
as his first gift to those who believe,
to complete his work on earth
and bring us the fullness of grace.

Invocation of the Holy Spirit
Father, may this Holy Spirit sanctify these offerings.
Let them become the body † and blood of Jesus Christ
    our Lord
as we celebrate the great mystery
which he left us as an everlasting covenant.

The Lord's Supper
He always loved those who were his own in the world.

When the time came for him to be glorified by you, his
     heavenly Father,
he showed the depth of his love.
While they were at supper,
he took bread, said the blessing, broke the bread
and gave it to his disciples, saying:
Take this, all of you, and eat it:
this is my body which will be given up for you.

In the same way, he took the cup, filled with wine.
He gave you thanks, and giving the cup to his
     disciples, said:

Take this, all of you, and drink from it:
this is the cup of my blood,
the blood of the new and everlasting covenant.
It will be shed for you and for all men
so that sins may be forgiven.
Do this in memory of me.

Memorial acclamation of the people
Let us proclaim the mystery of faith:
1. **Christ has died,**
   Christ is risen,
   Christ will come again.
2. **Dying you destroyed our death,**
   rising you restored our life.
   Lord Jesus, come in glory.
3. **When we eat this bread and drink this cup,**
   we proclaim your death, Lord Jesus,
   until you come in glory.
4. **Lord, by your cross and resurrection**
   you have set us free.
   You are the Saviour of the world.

The memorial prayer
Father, we now celebrate this memorial of our
    redemption.
We recall Christ's death, his descent among the dead,
his resurrection, and his ascension to your right hand;
and, looking forward to his coming in glory,
we offer you his body and blood,
the acceptable sacrifice
which brings salvation to the whole world.

Intercessions for the Church
Lord, look upon this sacrifice which you have given to
    your Church;
and by your Holy Spirit, gather all who share this one
    bread and one cup
into the one body of Christ, a living sacrifice of praise.

Lord, remember those for whom we offer this sacrifice,
especially N. our Pope,
N. our bishop, and bishops and clergy everywhere.
Remember those who take part in this offering,
those here present and all your people,
and all who seek you with a sincere heart.

For the dead
Remember those who have died in the peace of Christ
and all the dead whose faith is known to you alone.

In communion with the saints
Father, in your mercy grant also to us, your children,
to enter into our heavenly inheritance
in the company of the Virgin Mary, the Mother of God,
and your apostles and saints.
Then, in your kingdom, freed from the corruption of
    sin and death,
we shall sing your glory with every creature through
    Christ our Lord,
through whom you give us everything that is good.

Final doxology: in praise of God
Through him,
with him,
in him,
in the unity of the Holy Spirit,
all glory and honour is yours,
almighty Father,
for ever and ever.
    Amen.

Communion Rite

All stand

THE LORD'S PRAYER
The priest invites us to join him in saying the Lord's
prayer, using the following or similar words.

Let us pray with confidence to the Father in the words
our Saviour gave us.

    Our Father, who art in heaven,
    hallowed be thy name;
    thy kingdom come;
    thy will be done on earth as it is in heaven.
    Give us this day our daily bread;
    and forgive us our trespasses
    as we forgive those who trespass against us;
    and lead us not into temptation,
    but deliver us from evil.

Deliver us, Lord, from every evil,
and grant us peace in our day.
In your mercy keep us free from sin
and protect us from all anxiety
as we wait in joyful hope
for the coming of our Saviour, Jesus Christ.

For the kingdom, the power, and the glory are yours, now and forever.

THE RITE OF PEACE

Lord Jesus Christ, you said to your apostles:
I leave you peace, my peace I give you.
Look not on our sins, but on the faith of your Church,
and grant us the peace and unity of your kingdom
where you live for ever and ever.
    Amen.
The peace of the Lord be with you always.
    And also with you.
The deacon (or priest) may add these or similar words.
Let us offer each other the sign of peace.
(All make an appropriate sign of peace according to
local custom.)

BREAKING OF BREAD

The priest breaks the host and places a small piece in
the chalice saying quietly:
May this mingling of the body and blood of our Lord
    Jesus Christ
bring eternal life to us who receive it.
During the breaking of bread the Lamb of God is either
sung or said.
    **Lamb of God, you take away the sins of the
    world:**
        have mercy on us.
    **Lamb of God, you take away the sins of the
    world:**
        have mercy on us.
    **Lamb of God, you take away the sins of the
    world:**
        grant us peace.

PREPARATION FOR COMMUNION

The priest prepares privately for communion.

Lord Jesus Christ, Son of the living God, by the will of the Father and the work of the Holy Spirit your death brought life to the world. By your holy body and blood free me from all my sins and from every evil. Keep me faithful to your teaching, and never let me be parted from you.

or

Lord Jesus Christ, with faith in your love and mercy I eat your body and drink your blood. Let it not bring me condemnation, but health in mind and body.

INVITATION TO COMMUNION

The priest invites the people to share communion.

This is the Lamb of God
who takes away the sins of the world.
Happy are those who are called to his supper.

> **Lord, I am not worthy to receive you,**
> **but only say the word and I shall be healed.**

After the priest has communicated, the congregation approach the altar to communicate. The communion hymn or antiphon may be sung or said during communion.

COMMUNION SONG: *Proper of the Day*

The body of Christ.
Amen.
For the chalice.
The blood of Christ.
Amen.

SILENCE OR SONG

After communion there follows a period of silence, or a hymn of praise or psalm may be sung.

PRAYER AFTER COMMUNION: *Proper of the Day*

All stand

Let us pray.
At the end of the prayer the people respond:
  Amen.

Concluding Rite

Greeting.
The Lord be with you.
  And also with you.
Blessing.
May almighty God bless you.
The Father, and the Son,† and the Holy Spirit.
  Amen.
[On certain days another solemn form of blessing or
prayer over the people may be used.]
Dismissal.
Go in the peace of Christ.
or
The Mass is ended, go in peace.
or
Go in peace to love and serve the Lord.
  Thanks be to God.

Prayers after Mass

To God the Father
We thank you, Father, that in this Mass you have
accepted our simple gifts of bread and wine and
transformed them into the body and blood of your
well-beloved Son, through the power of your Holy
Spirit. Take our lives and transform them so that we
may live as bread that is broken and scattered on the
hills to feed our hungry world. We make this prayer
through Christ our Lord. Amen.

Michael Buckley

94

To the Holy Spirit

Spirit of the living God, you have fallen on us afresh at Mass and filled us with your saving grace, may we now, filled with your spirit witness to the new life within us and so draw all, with whom we come in contact, into union with you and so give honour and praise to God our Father. Amen.

Michael Buckley

For sharing

Lord Jesus Christ, you have come to us and shared your life and resurrection with us in this holy Mass; supported by your example and nourished with your body and blood, may we share with others the truth of your gospel and the power of your intercession for all mankind. Amen.

Michael Buckley

For peace

Lord Jesus Christ, at Mass you have given us your peace, show us then the peace we should seek, the peace we must give, the peace we can keep and the peace we must forgo so that your life may be lived in us as a sign of your love for everyone to see and experience. Amen.

Michael Buckley

For the church

O God, our refuge, and our strength, look down in mercy on your people who cry to you; and by the intercession of the glorious and immaculate virgin Mary, mother of God, of Saint Joseph her spouse, of your blessed apostles Peter and Paul and of all the saints, in mercy and goodness hear our prayers for the conversion of sinners, and for the liberty and exaltation of our holy mother the Church. Through Christ our Lord. Amen.

The Sacrament

Prayers before Holy Communion

Almighty and ever living God,
I approach the sacrament of your only-begotten Son,
our Lord Jesus Christ.
I come sick to the doctor of life,
unclean to the fountain of mercy,
blind to the radiance of eternal light,
and poor and needy to the Lord of heaven and earth.
Lord, in your great generosity,
heal my sickness, wash away my defilement,
enlighten my blindness, enrich my poverty,
and clothe my nakedness.
May I receive the bread of angels,
the King of kings and Lord of lords,
with humble reverence,
with the purity and faith,
the repentance and love, and the determined purpose
that will help to bring me to salvation.
May I receive the sacrament of the Lord's body and
    blood,
and its reality and power.
Kind God,
may I receive the body of your only-begotten Son,
our Lord Jesus Christ,
born from the womb of the Virgin Mary,
and so be received into his mystical body,
and numbered among his members.
Loving Father,
as on my earthly pilgrimage

I now receive your beloved Son
under the veil of a sacrament,
may I one day see him face to face in glory,
who lives and reigns with you for ever. Amen.

Saint Thomas Aquinas

Give me, good Lord, a full faith and a fervent charity,
a love of you, good Lord,
    incomparable above the love of myself;
and that I love nothing to your displeasure but
    everything in an order to you.

Take from me, good Lord, this lukewarm fashion,
    or rather
cold manner of meditation
    and this dullness in praying to you.
And give me warmth, delight and life in thinking
    about you.
And give me your grace to long for your holy
    sacraments
and specially to rejoice in the presence of your blessed
    body, sweet
Saviour Christ, in the holy sacrament of the altar, and
    duly to thank you for your gracious coming.

Saint Thomas More

Lord Jesus Christ,
I approach your banquet table
in fear and trembling,
for I am a sinner,
and dare not rely on my own worth,
but only on your goodness and mercy.
I am defiled by many sins in body and soul,
and by my unguarded thoughts and words.

Gracious God of majesty and awe,
I seek your protection,
I look for your healing.
Poor troubled sinner that I am,
I appeal to you, the fountain of all mercy.
I cannot bear your judgment,
but I trust in your salvation.
Lord, I show my wounds to you
and uncover my shame before you.
I know my sins are many and great,
and they fill me with fear,
but I hope in your mercies,
for they cannot be numbered.

Lord Jesus Christ, eternal king, God and man,
crucified for mankind,
look upon me with mercy and hear my prayer,
for I trust in you.
Have mercy on me,
full of sorrow and sin,
for the depth of your compassion never ends.
Praise to you, saving sacrifice,
offered on the wood of the cross for me and for all
    mankind.
Praise to the noble and precious blood,
flowing from the wounds of my crucified
    Lord Jesus Christ
and washing away the sins of the whole world.
Remember, Lord, your creature,
whom you have redeemed with your blood.
I repent my sins,
and I long to put right what I have done.

Merciful Father, take away all my offences and sins;
purify me in body and soul,
and make me worthy to taste the holy of holies.
May your body and blood,

which I intend to receive, although I am unworthy,
be for me the remission of my sins,
the washing away of my guilt,
the end of my evil thoughts,
and the rebirth of my better instincts.
May it incite me to do the works pleasing to you
and profitable to my health in body and soul,
and be a firm defence
against the wiles of my enemies.
Amen.

Saint Ambrose

Sancti, venite

Draw nigh and take the body of the Lord,
and drink the holy blood for you outpoured.
Saved by that body and that holy blood,
with souls refreshed, we render thanks to God.
Mankind is ransomed from eternal loss
by flesh and blood offered upon the cross.
Salvation's giver, Christ, the only Son,
by his dear cross and blood the victory won.
Offered was he for greatest and for least,
himself the victim, and himself the priest.
Victims are offered by the law of old,
which in a type this heavenly mystery told.
He, ransomer from death, and light from shade,
now gives his holy grace his saints to aid.
Approach ye then with faithful hearts sincere,
and take the safeguard of salvation here.
He, that his saints in this world rules and shields,
to all believers life eternal yields;
With heavenly bread makes them that hunger whole,
gives living waters to the thirsting soul. Amen.

Bangor Antiphonary

Father, all-powerful and ever-living God,
we do well always and everywhere to give you thanks
through Jesus Christ our Lord.
At the last supper,
as he sat at table with his apostles,
he offered himself to you as the spotless lamb,
the acceptable gift that gives you perfect praise.
Christ has given us this memorial of his passion
to bring us its saving power until the end of time.
In this great sacrament you feed your people
and strengthen them in holiness,
so that the family of mankind
may come to walk in the light of one faith,
in one communion of love.
We come then to this wonderful sacrament
to be fed at your table
and grow into the likeness of the risen Christ.
Earth unites with heaven
to sing the new song of creation
as we adore and praise you for ever.

Preface of Corpus Christi

My God, and is thy table spread,
and does thy cup with love o'erflow?
Thither be all thy children led,
and let them all thy sweetness know.

Hail, sacred feast, which Jesus makes!
Rich banquet of his flesh and blood!
Thrice happy he, who here partakes
that sacred stream, that heavenly food.

O let thy table honoured be,
and furnished well with joyful guests;
and may each soul salvation see,
that here its sacred pledges tastes.

Philip Doddridge

Act of faith in the real presence

Lord Jesus Christ, I believe you are as truly present in
this holy sacrament, under the signs of bread and
wine, as you were when dying upon a cross for the
salvation of all mankind, or as you are now enthroned
in glory in heaven at the right hand of the Father. You
said that you would give us yourself as the bread of
life, which if we eat, we shall live forever. I believe this
truth because you are truth itself. With confidence in
your loving forgiveness therefore, I approach your
altar, conscious that my unworthiness to receive you is
outweighed by your desire to be united with my soul.
You desire to nourish it on its earthly pilgrimage, until
the day when I shall be with you in the eternal
banquet, to feed on the unveiled beauty of your
presence forever.

Our Lady

Most blessed Virgin Mary, who under the shadow and
power of the Holy Spirit prepared in your spotless
womb a fit dwelling place for the Incarnate Word of
God, intercede for me now so that, by the power of the
same Holy Spirit, I may be purified and become less
unworthy to receive my Lord and Saviour under my
roof.

Act of spiritual communion (when unable to receive the sacrament)

My Jesus, I believe that you are truly present in the
most blessed sacrament. I love you above all things,

and I desire to possess you within my soul. Since I am unable now to receive you sacramentally, come at least spiritually into my heart. I embrace you as if you were already there, and I unite myself wholly to you; never permit me to be separated from you.

Saint Alphonsus

Prayers after Holy Communion

I give you thanks,
Lord, holy Father, everlasting God.
In your great mercy,
and not because of my own merits,
you have fed me, a sinner and your unworthy servant,
with the precious body and blood of your Son,
our Lord Jesus Christ.

I pray that this holy communion
may not serve as my judgment and condemnation,
but as my forgiveness and salvation.

May it be my armour of faith
and shield of good purpose.
May it root out in me all vice and evil desires,
increase my love and patience,
humility and obedience,
and every virtue.

Make it a firm defence
against the wiles of all my enemies, seen and unseen,
while restraining all evil impulses of flesh and spirit.
May it help me to cleave to you, the one true God,
and bring me a blessed death when you call.

I beseech you to bring me, a sinner,
to that glorious feast where,
with your Son and Holy Spirit,
you are the true light of your holy ones,

their flawless blessedness,
everlasting joy,
and perfect happiness.
Through Christ our Lord. Amen.

Saint Thomas Aquinas

Prayer before a crucifix

Behold, O kind and most sweet Jesus, I cast myself on
my knees in your sight, and with the most fervent
desire of my soul, I pray and beseech you that you
would impress upon my heart lively sentiments of
faith, hope and charity, with a true repentance for my
sins and a firm desire of amendment, while with deep
affection and grief of soul I ponder within myself and
mentally contemplate your five most precious
wounds, having before my eyes that which David
spoke in prophecy of you, O good Jesus: 'They pierced
my hands and my feet; they have numbered all my
bones.'

Anima Christi

Soul of Christ, sanctify me.
Body of Christ, save me.
Blood of Christ, fill me.
Water from the side of Christ, wash me.
Passion of Christ, strengthen me.
O good Jesus, hear me.
Within your wounds hide me.
Suffer me not to be separated from you.
From the malicious enemy defend me.
In the hour of my death call me.
And bid me come unto you.
That with your saints I may praise you.
For ever and ever.

Early fourteenth century prayer

For reverence

Lord Jesus, who in this wonderful sacrament has left us a memorial of your passion: grant us, we beseech you, so to reverence the sacred mysteries of your body and blood, that we may always feel in our souls the fruit of your redemption. Who lives and reigns, God, world without end.

Desire for closer union

Lord Jesus Christ, pierce my soul with your love so that I may always long for you alone, who are the bread of angels and the fulfilment of the soul's deepest desires. May my heart always hunger and feed upon you, so that my soul may be filled with the sweetness of your presence. May my soul thirst for you, who are the source of life, wisdom, knowledge, light and all the riches of God our Father. May I always seek and find you, think upon you, speak to you and do all things for the honour and glory of your holy name. Be always my only hope, my peace, my refuge and my help in whom my heart is rooted so that I may never be separated from you.

Saint Bonaventure

Fruits of the passion

Most sweet Jesus Christ, grant that your passion may be to me a power by which I am strengthened, protected and defended. May your wounds be to me food and drink by which I am nourished and sustained. May the sprinkling of your blood be to me an ablution for all my sins. May your death prove to me life everlasting and may your cross be to me an eternal glory. May your resurrection be my sure hope of future glory. In these be my refreshment, my joy, my preservation and sweetness of heart.

For Mary's assistance

Most Holy Mary, with confidence in your intercession, I ask your prayers that I may always have a great devotion to your Son in the blessed sacrament and that as he has given himself to me so may I dedicate my life to his love and service.

For frequent reception of Holy Communion

Loving Lord Jesus, who came into the world to bring the life of grace to those who believe in you, and who foster it in daily communion, we humbly ask you to pour upon us all the gifts of the Holy Spirit. May those who have neglected you turn to you, and long to receive you in holy communion, and may we, who today received your body and blood, learn to approach your sacred banquet daily with devotion, where we will receive the remedy for all our faults, and be so nourished with the life of your grace that we may come at last to the happiness of life with you at your eternal banquet.

Prayers before the Blessed Sacrament

Prayer of love for a holy hour

Most sweet Jesus, I believe that you are as truly present here in the tabernacle as when you walked in Galilee where you ministered to the sick, the lame and the blind. Your ears of mercy were ever open to listen to the cries of the sorrowing and wounded and your lips ever ready to speak words of sympathy, comfort and encouragement to those who trusted in your power to help them.

As a sinner conscious of your mercy I come before you now to spend an hour in communion with you. Too long have I heard your plea 'could you not watch one hour with me?', and too long have I neglected to respond to it. Now at last I come to you, Jesus, my patient and faithful friend, to whom I can open my heart as someone who fully understands me.

Sweet Jesus, you know me better than I know myself. You perceive the innermost secrets of my heart and see there my longing to be totally yours. Deep down within me I want to love you, but at the same time I am aware of the promptings of my sinful nature drawing me away from you, and the unselfish service which I should render to you. Jesus, I have asked, and now ask you again to make me love you in spite of my weaker self. Fill each day of my life with acts of love for you and make me realise what your love really means. Enlighten my understanding that I may clearly see that to love you means wealth beyond measure and to serve you reward without limit. Sweet heart of Jesus I implore that I may love you daily more and more.

Adoro te devote
Godhead here in hiding, whom I do adore
Masked by these bare shadows, shape and nothing
  more,
See, Lord, at thy service low lies here a heart
Lost, all lost in wonder at the God thou art.

Seeing, touching, tasting are in thee deceived;
How says trusty hearing? That shall be believed;
What God's Son has told me, take for truth I do;
Truth himself speaks truly or there's nothing true.

On the cross thy godhead made no sign to men;
Here thy very manhood steals from human ken:
Both are my confession, both are my belief,
And I pray the prayer of the dying thief.

I am not like Thomas, wounds I cannot see,
But can plainly call thee Lord and God as he:

This faith each day deeper be my holding of,
Daily make me harder hope and dearer love.

O thou our reminder of Christ crucified,
Living Bread the life of us for whom he died,
Lend this life to me then: feed and feast my mind,
There be thou the sweetness man was meant to find.

Bring the tender tale true of the Pelican;
Bathe me, Jesu Lord, in what thy bosom ran –
Blood that but one drop of has the worth to win
All the world forgiveness of its world of sin.

Jesu whom I look at shrouded here below,
I beseech thee send me what I thirst for so,
Some day to gaze on thee face to face in light
And be blest for ever with thy glory's sight.

Gerard Manley Hopkins

In silence
To be there before you Lord, that's all
To shut the eyes of my body,
To shut the eyes of my soul,
And to be still and silent,
To expose myself to you who are there, exposed to me.
To be there before you, the Eternal Presence.
I am willing to feel nothing, Lord,
        to see nothing
        to hear nothing.
Empty of all ideas
        of all images,
In the darkness.
Here I am, simply
To meet you without obstacles,
In the silence of faith,
Before you, Lord.

Michel Quoist

Sweet heart of Jesus,
    fount of love and mercy,
today we come,
    thy blessing to implore;
O touch our hearts,
    so cold and so ungrateful,
and make them, Lord,
    thine own for evermore.

Sweet heart of Jesus, we implore,
O make us love thee more and more.

Sweet heart of Jesus,
    make us know and love thee,
unfold to us
    the treasures of thy grace;
that so our hearts,
    from things of earth uplifted,
may long alone
    to gaze upon thy face.

Sweet heart of Jesus,
    make us pure and gentle,
and teach us how
    to do thy blessed will;
to follow close
    the print of thy dear footsteps,
and when we fall
    sweet heart, oh, love us still.

Sweet heart of Jesus,
    bless all hearts that love thee,
and may thine own
    heart ever blessed be;
bless us, dear Lord,
    and bless the friends we cherish,
and keep us true
    to Mary and to thee.

Traditional

Seeking a blessing

My Jesus, take from my heart all that displeases you and bless me as you blessed your disciples before ascending into heaven. May this blessing change me, fill me with your Holy Spirit, and be an assured pledge of the final benediction which you will bestow on me and all your elect on the last day.

Food for service

O Jesus, present in the sacrament of the altar, teach all the nations to serve you with willing hearts, knowing that to serve God is to reign. May your sacrament, O Jesus, be light to the mind, strength to the will, joy to the heart. May it be the support of the weak, the comfort of the suffering, the wayfaring bread of salvation for the dying and for all the pledge of future glory.

Pope John XXIII

Support for families

O living bread, that came down from heaven to give life to the world! O loving shepherd of our souls, from your throne of glory whence, a 'hidden God', you pour out your grace on families and peoples, we commend to you particularly the sick, the unhappy, the poor and all who beg for food and employment, imploring for all and every one the assistance of your providence; we commend to you the families, so that they may be fruitful centres of Christian life. May the abundance of your grace be poured out over all.

Pope John XXIII

Act of consecration

Lord Jesus Christ, who for love of us remains night and day in this sacrament, full of kindness and love, awaiting, inviting and welcoming all who come to visit you: I believe that you are present in the sacrament of the altar. I adore you from the depth of my own nothingness, and I thank you for all the graces which you have granted me. I thank you especially for having given yourself to me in this sacrament; for having given me your own most holy mother, Mary, for my advocate; and for having called me to visit you in this church. I pay homage this day to your adorable heart and desire to do so for three ends: firstly, in thanksgiving for this great gift; secondly, to make reparation for all the injuries which you have received in this sacrament from your enemies; and thirdly, I desire to adore you, through this visit, in all the places on earth where your sacramental presence is least honoured and most neglected. My Jesus, I love you with my whole heart. I am sorry for having offended your infinite goodness so many times in the past. I resolve, with the help of your grace, never to offend you more for the time to come; and at this present moment I consecrate myself completely to you. I give to you, withholding nothing, all my own will, my inclinations, my desires, everything that is mine. From this day forward, do with me and with what belongs to me as it shall please you. All that I ask and desire is your holy love, final perseverance and the perfect fulfilment of your will. I commend to you the souls in purgatory, particularly those who were most devoted to the blessed sacrament and to Mary, your holy mother. I commend to you, too, all poor sinners.

And now, dear Saviour, I join all my desires with the desires of your loving heart; I offer them to your eternal Father, and I beg him in your name, and for your love, to accept them and fulfil them.

Paul's prayer

Out of his infinite glory, may he give you the power
through his Spirit for your hidden self to grow strong,
so that Christ may live in your hearts through faith,
and then, planted in love and built on love, you will
with all the saints have strength to grasp the breadth
and the length, the height and the depth, until,
knowing the love of Christ, which is beyond all
knowledge, you are filled with the utter fullness of
God. Glory be to him whose power, working in us, can
do infinitely more than we can ask or imagine; glory be
to him from generation to generation in the Church
and in Christ Jesus for ever and ever. Amen.

Ephesians 3:16–21

Jesus, my Lord, my God, my all,
how can I love thee as I ought?
And how revere this wondrous gift,
so far surpassing hope or thought?

Sweet sacrament, we thee adore;
Oh, make us love thee more and more.

Had I but Mary's sinless heart
to love thee with, my dearest King,
Oh, with what bursts of fervent praise
thy goodness, Jesus, would I sing!

Ah, see! within a creature's hand
the vast Creator deigns to be,
reposing, infant-like, as though
on Joseph's arm, or Mary's knee.

Thy body, soul, and Godhead, all;
O mystery of love divine!
I cannot compass all I have,
for all thou hast and art are mine.

Sound, sound, his praises higher still,
and come, ye angels, to our aid;
'tis God, 'tis God, the very God
whose power both man and angels made.

Frederick William Faber

Act of trust

Lord Jesus, I believe in your presence on the altar; help my unbelief. I trust my life to you; fill up my lack of confidence. I love you: warm my cold heart which seeks comfort elsewhere. Accept my faith, hope and love such as they are, and through the power of your sacred presence make up for what is lacking so that I may know, trust and serve you this and every day of my life.

Act of love

You know better than I how much I love you, Lord. You know it and I know it not, for nothing is more hidden from me than the depths of my own heart. I desire to love you; I fear that I do not love you enough. I beseech you to grant me the fullness of pure love. Behold my desire; you have given it to me. Behold in your creature what you have placed there. O God, who love me enough to inspire me to love you for ever, behold not my sins. Behold your mercy and my love.

For/the fullness of love

Set our hearts on fire with love to thee, O Christ our God, that in that flame we may love thee with all our hearts, with all our minds, with all our souls, and with all our strength, and our neighbours as ourselves; so that, keeping thy commandments, we may glorify thee, the giver of all good gifts.

Prayer of abandonment

Be thou a light unto my eyes, music to mine ears,
sweetness to my taste, and full contentment to my
heart. Be thou my sunshine in the day, my food at
table, my repose in the night, my clothing in
nakedness, and my succour in all necessities, Lord
Jesu, I give thee my body, my soul, my substance, my
frame, my friends, my liberty and my life. Dispose of
me and all that is mine as it may seem best to thee and
to the glory of thy blessed name. Amen.

A light to others

My Lord and my God,
thank you for drawing me to yourself.
Make me desire more deeply
that knowledge of you which is eternal life.
Lord, you have told us that the pure in heart shall see
God – the single-minded
who do not try to serve two masters,
who have no other gods but you.
Keep the burning of my desire for you
as clear and steady as the flame of a candle
– a single, undivided focus of attention,
a steady offering of the will.
Let my whole being be filled with your light
so that others may be drawn to you.
Let my whole being be cleansed
by the flame of your love
from all that is contrary to your will for me,
from all that keeps others from coming to you.
Let my whole being be consumed in your service,
so that others may know your love,
– my Lord and my God.

An instrument of love

Use me, my Saviour, for whatever purpose and in whatever way thou mayest require. Here is my poor heart, an empty vessel; fill it with thy grace. Here is my sinful, troubled soul; quicken it and refresh it with thy love. Take my heart for thine abode; my mouth to spread abroad the glory of thy name; my love and all my powers for the advancement of thy believing people, and never suffer the steadfastness and confidence of my faith to abate.

Aspirations
(when genuflecting before the reserved sacrament)

My Lord and my God.

O sacrament most holy, O sacrament divine,
All praise and all thanksgiving be every moment thine.

O heart of Jesus in the blessed sacrament, burning with love for us, inflame our hearts with love for thee.

May the heart of Jesus in the most blessed sacrament be praised, adored and loved, with grateful affection at every moment, in all the tabernacles of the world, even to the end of time.

Adoration
My Jesus, I adore you present on the altar for love of me: grant that I may love you more and more.

Thanksgiving
My Jesus, I thank you with all my heart for your loving kindness to me. Blessed and praised every moment be the most holy and divine sacrament.

Offering

My Jesus, in the most holy sacrament you have given yourself to me: accept in return all the senses of my body and all the faculties of my soul. Give me light and grace: light to know your holy will and grace to do it.

Gift

Lord Jesus, I give you my body, my soul, my possessions and friends, all that I am and have. Dispose of them according to your will and to the glory of your name.

Sorrow

My Jesus, too often have I offended you, and now before you in the blessed sacrament I ask the grace never to sin again.

Eucharistic Exposition and Benediction

The structure of the Rite is as follows:
> Exposition
> Adoration
> Benediction
> Reposition

Exposition

O salutaris hostia,
Quae caeli pandis ostium;
Bella premunt hostilia,
Da robur, fer auxilium.

Uni Trinoque Domino
Sit sempiterna gloria,
Qui vitam sine termino
Nobis donet in patria.
Amen.

or
O saving victim, opening wide
the gate of heaven to man below;
our foes press on from every side;
your aid supply, your strength bestow.

To your great name be endless praise,
immortal Godhead, one in three;
O grant us endless length of days
in our true native land with thee. Amen.

Adoration
Prayers, readings and songs assist our worship of
Christ, our Lord.

Benediction
Tantum ergo Sacramentum
Veneremur cernui:
Et antiquum documentum
Novo cedat ritui:
Praestet fides supplementum
Sensuum defectui.

Genitori, Genitoque
Laus et jubilatio,
Salus, honor, virtus quoque
Sit et benedictio;
Procedenti ab utroque
Compar sit laudatio.
Amen.
or
Therefore we, before him bending,
this great sacrament revere;
types and shadows have their ending,
for the newer rite is here;
faith our outward sense befriending,
makes the inward vision clear.

Glory let us give, and blessing
to the Father and the Son;
honour, might, and praise addressing,
while eternal ages run;
ever too his love confessing,
who, from both, with both is one.
Amen.

The minister may lead us in one or more of the
following prayers:
For your gift of the eucharist,
through which we proclaim the Lord's death until he
comes again:
    God, Our Father, we bless you.
For the gift of the eucharist,
through which you give us strength and satisfy our
hunger:
    God, Our Father, we bless you.
For your gift of the eucharist,
through which all your children are brought together
in brotherly love:
    God, Our Father, we bless you.

You are the bread of life:
    Praise to you.
You are the bread of salvation:
    Praise to you.
You are the blood that redeemed us:
    Praise to you.
You are the source of our joy:
    Praise to you.
You are the bread that feeds us:
    Praise to you.
You are the blood that quenches our thirst:
    Praise to you.

You are the bread that comforts us:
   Praise to you.
You are the bread that gives us strength:
   Praise to you.
You are the bread that heals us in body and mind:
   Praise to you.

Lord Jesus Christ,
you gave us the eucharist
as the memorial of your suffering and death.
May our worship of this sacrament of your body and
   blood
help us to experience the salvation you won for us
and the peace of the kingdom
where you live with the Father and the Holy Spirit,
one God, for ever and ever. **Amen.**
or
Lord our God,
in this great sacrament
we come into the presence of Jesus Christ, your Son,
born of the virgin Mary
and crucified for our salvation.
May we who declare our faith in this fountain of love
   and mercy
drink from it the water of everlasting life. **Amen.**
or
Lord our God,
may we always give due honour
to the sacramental presence of the Lamb who was slain
   for us.
May our faith be rewarded
by the vision of his glory,
who lives and reigns for ever and ever. **Amen.**
or
Lord our God,
you have given us the true bread from heaven.

In the strength of this food
may we live always by your life
and rise in glory on the last day. **Amen.**
or
Lord,
give to our hearts
the light of faith and the fire of love,
that we may worship in spirit and in truth
our God and Lord, present in this sacrament,
who lives and reigns for ever and ever. **Amen.**
or
Lord,
may this sacrament of new life
warm our hearts with your love
and make us eager
for the eternal joy of your kingdom. **Amen.**
or
Lord our God,
teach us to cherish in our hearts
the paschal mystery of your Son
by which you redeemed the world.
Watch over the gifts of grace
your love has given us
and bring them to fulfilment
in the glory of heaven. **Amen.**

Reposition
Adoremus in aeternum sanctissimum Sacramentum.
Laudate Dominum, omnes gentes;
laudate eum omnes populi.

Quoniam confirmata est super nos misericordia ejus;
et veritas Domini manet in aeternum.

Gloria Patri, et Filio,
et Spiritui Sancto.

Sicut erat in principio, et nunc, et semper,
et in saecula saeculorum. Amen.
Adoremus in aeternum sanctissimum Sacramentum.

Let us adore for ever the most holy Sacrament.
O praise the Lord, all you nations;
praise him, all you people.
For his mercy is confirmed upon us;
and the truth of the Lord remains for ever.
Glory be to the Father, and to the Son,
and to the Holy Spirit.
As it was in the beginning, is now,
and ever shall be, world without end. Amen.
Let us adore for ever the most holy Sacrament.

Reconciliation

Jesus Christ is the reconciler between us and God. By his wounds we are healed, when through sin we stray from the path which leads to union with God our Father: God in Christ was reconciling the world to himself, not holding men's faults against them. 2 Corinthians 5:19. Just as the eucharist is the most perfect form of the celebration of our loving union with God in Christ, so the sacrament of reconciliation is the most privileged form of Christ forgiving us our offences against God, our neighbour and ourselves.

We give and receive forgiveness within the Church, as members of Christ's body, so that, in common with all the sacraments, reconciliation is essentially a 'Church' sacrament. It is a community action. While individual confession is still required, nevertheless the Christian community dimension is never forgotten. When we sin the whole body suffers; when we repent and are reconciled, the whole body increases in holiness and grace. We are not alone in sinning or being reconciled. In order to understand this sacrament we need to appreciate the three-dimensional nature of sin. Sin divides us from God, from each other, and sets up a conflict within ourselves as individuals.

1. *Alienation from God* Sin means that we refuse to give our Father the loving obedience which is his due.
2. *Division among people* Every sin harms the community, at least indirectly, in that it introduces disorder into people's attitude and conduct.

3. *Disintegration of the individual* Sin disturbs the balance between the two poles – love of God and our neighbour – which should direct our lives.

If sin is abandoning the Father's house, then repentance is returning to it. The mission of Christ and the Church is a mission of repentance. *Repent and believe the gospel* is the keynote and driving force of the sacrament of reconciliation. The reading of God's word in the celebration of the sacrament calls forth our response, by which we are healed and reconciled. Reconciliation is a gospel and community-based sacrament.

The three aspects of repentance cancel out the three-dimensional nature of our sin.

1. *Conversion to God* We admit our sin, recognise we are not worthy of God's love, but, trusting in the merits of Christ, we throw ourselves on the mercy of God.
2. *Reconciliation with the community* To the community we have offended we return in love and reparation.
3. *Integration of self* Conversion gradually purifies us so that we may more perfectly love God and our neighbour as ourselves.

The sacrament of reconciliation is today more frequently being celebrated in the community setting of penitential services. In every celebration, whether individually or collectively, Christ's reconciling, healing power is at work in the Church.

Prayers before the Sacrament of Reconciliation

God the Father

Almighty and most merciful God, who made me out of nothing and redeemed me by the precious blood of your only Son, I humbly ask you to forgive my sins. I desire most sincerely to forsake all my evil ways in which I have lost my true self. With the prodigal son in the gospel story I desire to think seriously about the direction of my life, and like him I resolve to return to my Father's house even though I am not worthy to be called your child. I know that you desire the conversion of the sinner, and that your mercy is above all your works. It is in this mercy that I place my trust, and as you have spared me so long and given me the desire of returning to you, so may you finish the work you have begun and bring me to full and perfect reconciliation with you.

I desire now to confess sincerely all my sins to you and your priest, and for this purpose I wish to know myself and call myself to account by a diligent examination of my conscience. But what will it avail to know my sins if you do not also give me the grace of sorrow and repentance? You insisted on a change of heart without which there can be no reconciliation and it is you alone who can bring about this change in me. Grant me, Father, this change of heart, as well as a lively faith and firm hope in the saving passion of your Son. I ask this through Christ, our Lord. Amen.

God the Son

Lord Jesus Christ, in your great love you wish that every sinner be converted and live in your grace. I grieve from the bottom of my heart that by my sins I have offended you, who shed your blood for me. May the same blood now plead for mercy for me before the face of God, our Father. For love of you I forgive all who have offended me and I firmly resolve to forsake every occasion of sin. I now sorrowfully confess all the sins I have committed against your divine goodness.

God the Holy Spirit
Come Holy Spirit, fill my heart with an awareness of your presence and kindle in me the fire of your love. Help me to discover my sins of commission and omission by which I have offended you and my neighbour. May I confess them with a humble and contrite heart, and by the help of your grace may I never sin again.

For true sorrow
O sweet Jesus, I grieve for my sins; vouchsafe to supply whatever is lacking to my true sorrow and to offer for me to God the Father all the grief which thou hast endured because of my sins and those of the whole world.

Saint Mechtilde

O Jesus, you who had no pity on yourself, you who are God, have pity on me who am a sinner.

Pierre Barbet

Our Lady
Holy virgin, mother of our Lord Jesus Christ, compassionate refuge of penitent sinners, by the sacred wounds of your Son, and the agony you felt as you stood by the foot of the cross, intercede for me now so that, sorrowful for my sins, I may humbly confess them, and live with your Son the life of the resurrection.

Guardian Angel and all the saints
O guardian angel sent to watch over me during my life be with me now in my sorrow for my sins. May my holy patron N. whose name I bear, Saint Peter, Saint Mary Magdalen and all the saints be my cloud of witnesses before the throne of God so that like the

prodigal son I may return to my Father's house never to leave it again.

The Penitential Psalms (excerpts)
It is a pious custom to recite the Seven Penitential Psalms as prayers against the seven deadly sins.

Psalm 6
Lord, do not reprove me in your anger;
punish me not in your rage.
Have mercy on me, Lord, I have no strength;
Lord, heal me, my body is racked;
my soul is racked with pain.

Psalm 31
Happy the man whose offence is forgiven,
whose sin is remitted.
But now I have acknowledged my sins;
my guilt I did not hide.
I said: 'I will confess
my offence to the Lord.
And you, Lord, have forgiven
the guilt of my sin.

Psalm 37
My wounds are foul and festering,
the result of my own folly.
I am bowed and brought to my knees.
I go mourning all the day long.
O Lord, you know all my longing:
my groans are not hidden from you.

Psalm 50
Have mercy on me, God, in your kindness.
In your compassion blot out my offence.
O wash me more and more from my guilt

And cleanse me from my sin
My offences truly I know them;
my sin is always before me.
Against you, you alone, have I sinned;
what is evil in your sight I have done.
O purify me, then I shall be clean;
O wash me, I shall be whiter than snow.

Psalm 101
O Lord, listen to my prayer
and let my cry for help reach you.
Do not hide your face from me
in the day of my distress.
Turn your ear towards me
and answer me quickly when I call.
My days are like a passing shadow
and I wither away like the grass.

Psalm 129
Out of the depths I cry to you, O Lord,
Lord, hear my voice!
O let your ears be attentive
to the voice of my pleading.
If you, O Lord, should mark our guilt,
Lord, who would survive?
But with you is found forgiveness:
for this we revere you.

Psalm 142
You are faithful, you are just; give answer
Do not call your servant to judgment
for no one is just in your sight.
For your name's sake, Lord, save my life;
in your justice save my soul from distress.

Before examination of conscience
Lord Jesus Christ, judge of the living and the dead,
before whom I must appear one day to give an exact
account of my whole life, enlighten me, I beseech you,
and give me a humble and contrite heart, that I may
see wherein I have offended your infinite majesty and
judge myself now with such a just severity that then
you may judge me with mercy and clemency.

After examination of conscience
My God, I detest these and all other sins which I have
committed against your divine majesty. I am sorry that
I have offended you, because you are infinitely good
and sin displeases you. I love you with my whole
heart, and firmly purpose by the help of your grace
never more to offend you. I resolve to avoid the
occasions of sin; I will confess my sins and endeavour
to make satisfaction for them. Have mercy on me, O
God, have mercy, and pardon me, a wretched sinner.
In the name of your beloved Son, Jesus, I humbly beg
you to wash me with his precious blood so that my
sins may be entirely remitted.

Prayers after the Sacrament of Reconciliation

To God the Father
Almighty and merciful God, I thank you that once
again you have welcomed me, your prodigal child,
despite the many times I have strayed from you.
Because of your tender mercies I now offer the rest of
my life to your service and renounce with my whole
soul all the offences I have committed against you. I
renew my baptismal promises and ask your grace that
in the future I may remain close to you, never to leave
you again.

To God the Son

Incarnate Word of God, who in your flesh reconciled all men to the Father, and continue to reconcile all those who in heartfelt sorrow confess their sins, I thank you that your healing power has touched me, and cleansed me from the leprosy of sin. Mercifully direct all my thoughts, words and actions to the greater glory of the Father, and be my model and help for the rest of my life so that I may persevere in your service and love.

To God the Holy Spirit

Holy Spirit, under whose guidance and inspiration I have confessed my sins, supply in me whatever is lacking in sorrow for my sins or purity of intention. Grant that the absolution pronounced on earth may be ratified in heaven, so that confident of your dwelling in me as in a holy temple, I may never defile it again but use it as a house of prayer, thanksgiving and service.

Our Lady, guardian angel and all the saints

O blessed Mary, my guardian angel and patron saint, Saint N. and all the saints give glory on my behalf to the blessed Trinity, for he who is mighty has done great things to me and holy is his name. Intercede for me before God's throne, so that when temptations come in the future, I may not dispute or compromise with them, but reject them absolutely lest I put the Lord our God to the test. May I be counted one day among the blessed in heaven, so that together with you I may praise God for his surpassing compassion and love.

In Thanksgiving
My soul, give thanks to the Lord,
All my being, bless his holy name.
My soul give thanks to the Lord
and never forget all his blessings.
It is he who forgives all your guilt,
who heals every one of your ills,
who redeems your life from the grave,
who crowns you with love and compassion,
who fills your life with good things,
renewing your youth like an eagle's.

Psalm 102

Prayer

Prayer is our birthright as Christians. It is God's gift to us and should be as 'natural' to us as breathing. All Christian prayer is identified with the risen Christ who in himself and for us has conquered sin, death and the power of the world over us. Since Christ prays through us we never pray alone because Christ's Spirit is one with our spirit. This is so because through baptism we are united with the risen Lord and by his Spirit we call God *Abba, Father!* Romans 8:16. His Spirit is one with ours. Prayer is, therefore, a loving relationship between God the Father and us. It is in the truest sense of the word a conversation between God within us and God around us. And all because Christ prays in us to his Father.

We believe that God is more ready to listen to us than we are to speak to him, ready to give infinitely more than we can ask or imagine. So we are truly praying when we listen to what he is saying to us in people, places and situations. Nothing is outside his love for us, even if it be suffering and death. The deepest prayer, therefore, is born of creative silence when God speaks to us of his will for our lives and their fulfilment.

There are some deep emotions of the Spirit which defy verbal expression: *The Spirit too comes to help us in our weakness. For when we cannot choose words in order to pray properly, the Spirit himself expresses our plea in a way that could never be put into words, and God who knows everything in our hearts knows perfectly well what he means.* Romans 8: 26–27.

Prayer is as varied and colourful as a rainbow. We may pray privately or in groups. From the earliest days of the Church the disciples of Jesus, as a group, used to pray, as was the Jewish custom, at certain hours of the day: *They went as a body to the Temple every day.* Acts 2:46.

Christ also said: *But when you pray, go to your private room and, when you have shut your door, pray to your Father who is in that secret place, and your Father who sees all that is done in secret will reward you.* Matthew 6:6. There is no substitute for personal prayer which bears the stamp of our individual and unique relationship with God. We may use set prayers, or prefer to speak spontaneously as the Spirit moves us. What is important is that they are born of the Spirit.

Prayer, even though dynamic and often defying analysis, is generally divided up into five categories: invocation, confession, thanksgiving, petition and intercession.

Invocation: we not only call God to be present to us but *remind ourselves* that God is always present to us when we call on his name.

Confession: we tell God of our sins of commission and omission.

Thanksgiving: we praise and thank God for his goodness in creation and redemption.

Petition: we ask God for the things we need for our life.

Intercession: we bring the wider needs of the Church and world to God who will provide for them.

All these forms of prayer, especially thanksgiving, are found in the Mass. The Spirit of the risen Christ takes all our prayers and offers them to the Father. In prayer we surrender our lives to his loving care. We can do nothing greater.

Because as Christians we are one in and with Christ through baptism, we are also in spiritual communion with each other. We belong to the communion of saints which embraces all those who are part of Christ's Church irrespective of time and space. The mother of Christ, the apostles, and all the holy men and women who, down through the ages, kept the flame of faith burning are the *great cloud* (of witnesses) *on every side of us*, Hebrews 12:1, which encourages us in our struggle on earth. We honour them because of their faithfulness to the gospel and because in a special way they are God's friends. They are part of our unseen community who join us in our prayers through Jesus Christ, his Son. Where they are, one day we hope to be, when we will join them and the angels in one triumphant hymn of praise to God our loving Father.

Daily Prayers

We should pray constantly *1 Thessalonians 5:18, so that* waking we may watch with Christ and sleeping we may rest in peace. *With minds and hearts fixed constantly on God then everything in our lives, whether in action or repose, is a hymn of praise and prayer. We may use reflection, aspirations, formal or spontaneous prayer as the Spirit moves us. All will be to the Father's glory.*

General Prayers

The Lord's Prayer
Our Father, who art in heaven,
hallowed be thy name;
thy kingdom come;
thy will be done on earth as it is in heaven.
Give us this day our daily bread;
and forgive us our trespasses,
as we forgive those that trespass against us;
and lead us not into temptation,
but deliver us from evil.
Amen.

The Hail Mary
Hail Mary, full of grace,
the Lord is with thee.
Blessed art thou among women,
and blessed is the fruit of thy womb, Jesus.
Holy Mary, Mother of God,
pray for us sinners, now,
and at the hour of our death.
Amen.

The Doxology
Glory be to the Father
and to the Son
and to the Holy Spirit.
As it was in the beginning
is now and ever shall be
world without end.
Amen.

The Apostles' Creed
I believe in God, the Father almighty, creator of
heaven and earth, and in Jesus Christ, his only Son,
our Lord, who was conceived by the Holy Spirit, born
of the Virgin Mary, suffered under Pontius Pilate, was
crucified, died, and was buried. He descended into
hell. The third day he rose again from the dead. He
ascended into heaven, sitteth at the right hand of God
the Father almighty. From thence he shall come to
judge the living and the dead. I believe in the Holy
Spirit, the holy Catholic Church, the Communion of
Saints, the forgiveness of sins, the resurrection of the
body, and life everlasting. Amen.

The Confiteor
I confess to almighty God, to blessed Mary, ever
virgin, to blessed Michael the archangel, to blessed
John the Baptist, to the holy apostles Peter and Paul,
and to all the saints, that I have sinned exceedingly in
thought, word and deed, through my fault, through
my fault, through my most grievous fault. Therefore I
beseech blessed Mary, ever virgin, blessed Michael the
archangel, blessed John the Baptist, the holy apostles
Peter and Paul, and all the saints to pray to the Lord
our God for me.

May almighty God have mercy on us, forgive us our
sins and bring us to life everlasting. Amen.

May the almighty and merciful Lord grant us pardon, absolution and remission of our sins. Amen.

Act of Contrition
O my God, I am sorry and beg pardon for all my sins, and detest them above all things, because they deserve your dreadful punishments, because they have crucified my loving Saviour Jesus Christ, and, most of all, because they offend your infinite goodness; and I firmly resolve, by the help of your grace, never to offend you again, and carefully to avoid the occasions of sin. Amen.

Prayer before the Acts
O almighty and eternal God, grant us an increase of faith, hope and charity: may we obtain what you have promised and make us love and practise what you command: through Jesus Christ our Lord. Amen.

Act of Faith
O my God, I firmly believe that you are the one only God, the creator and sovereign Lord of heaven and earth, infinitely great and infinitely good. I firmly believe that in you, one only God, there are three divine persons, really distinct and equal in all things, the Father, the Son and the Holy Ghost. I firmly believe that Jesus Christ, God the Son, became man; and he was conceived by the Holy Spirit and was born of the Virgin Mary; and he suffered and died on the cross to redeem and save us; that he arose the third day from the dead; and he ascended into heaven; and he will come at the end of the world to judge mankind; and that he will reward the good with eternal happiness and condemn the wicked to the everlasting pains of hell. I believe these, and all other articles which the holy Roman Catholic Church proposes to

our belief, because you, my God, the infallible truth, revealed them, and have commanded us to hear the Church, which is the pillar and the ground of truth. In this faith I am firmly resolved, by your holy grace, to live and die. Amen.

Act of Hope

My God, who has graciously promised every blessing, even heaven itself, through Jesus Christ, to those who keep your commandments. Relying on your infinite power, goodness, and mercy, and confiding in your sacred promises, to which you are always faithful, I confidently hope to obtain pardon of all my sins, grace to serve you faithfully in this life, by doing the good works you have commanded, which, with your assistance, I will perform; and eternal happiness in the next, through my Lord and Saviour Jesus Christ. Amen.

Act of Charity

My God, I love you with my whole heart and soul, and above all things, because you are infinitely good and perfect, and most worthy of all my love; and for your sake I love my neighbour as myself. Mercifully grant, O my God, that having loved you on earth, I may love and enjoy you for ever in heaven. Amen.

Short Acts

Act of Faith

O God, I firmly believe all the truths that you have revealed and that you teach us through your Church, for you are truth itself and can neither deceive nor be deceived.

Act of Hope

O God, I hope with complete trust that you will give me, through the merits of Jesus Christ, all necessary grace in this world and everlasting life in the world to come, for this is what you have promised and you always keep your promises.

Act of Charity

O God, I love you with my whole heart above all things, because you are infinitely good; and for your sake I love my neighbour as I love myself.

Act of Contrition

O God, I am sorry with my whole heart for all my sins because you are goodness itself and sin is an offence against you. Therefore I firmly resolve, with the help of your grace, not to sin again and to avoid the occasion of sin.

At the day's beginning

TO THE HOLY TRINITY

Most Holy Trinity, your goodness has brought me to the beginning of this day and now I offer it to you with its thoughts, words and actions together with any crosses and contradictions which I may encounter. Give your blessing to this day, your gift to me, so that it may be animated with your love and so bring glory and honour to your divine majesty. Amen.

Glory be to the Father who, when I did not exist created me by his power in the likeness of his own image; **and to the Son** who when I was lost redeemed me by his precious blood, **and to the Holy Spirit** who by his grace and goodness justified me in baptism, and many times afterwards when I had fallen. For each and all these benefits be the glory as great **as it was in the beginning**, and still greater be **now** in the course of

this present life, **and ever shall be** to the
consummation of the world and **world without end.
Amen.**

*As I recite this doxology I wish to offer to the Holy Trinity all
praise and I shall endeavour by grace to live this praise in
action throughout this day and for the rest of my life.*

TO GOD THE FATHER

Father,
I abandon myself into your hands;
do with me what you will.
Whatever you may do I thank you:
I am ready for all, I accept all.

Let only your will be done in me,
and in all your creatures.
I wish no more than this, O Lord.

Into your hands I commend my soul:
I offer it to you
with all the love of my heart,
for I love you, Lord,
and so need to give myself,
to surrender myself into your hands,
without reserve,
and with boundless confidence,
for you are my Father.

Charles de Foucauld

Into your hands, O Lord, we commend ourselves this
day. Let your presence be with us to its close.
Strengthen us to remember that in whatsoever good
work we do we are serving you. Give us a diligent and
watchful spirit, that we may seek in all things to know
your will, and knowing it, gladly to perform it, to the
honour and glory of your name; through Jesus Christ
our Lord.

Gelasian Sacramentary

O gracious and Holy Father, give us wisdom to perceive you, diligence to seek you, patience to wait for you, eyes to behold you, a heart to meditate upon you, and a life to proclaim you; through the power of the Spirit of Jesus Christ our Lord.

Saint Benedict

Eternal God, who are the light of the minds that know you, the joy of the hearts that love you, and the strength of the wills that serve you; grant us so to know you, that we may truly love you, and so to love you that we may fully serve you, whom to serve is perfect freedom, in Jesus Christ our Lord.

Saint Augustine

My God, I firmly believe that you are here and see me perfectly, and that you observe all my actions, all my thoughts, and the most secret movements of my heart. You permit me a sinner, who has so often offended you, to remain in your presence, and it is your goodness and bounty which command me to come to you. Give me grace, therefore, to pray as I should, and send your Holy Spirit upon me to kindle in my heart the fire of your love.

Heavenly Father, I offer you the life and death of your Son, and with them my affections and resolutions, my thoughts, words, deeds and sufferings this day and all my life, to honour your adorable majesty, to thank you for all your benefits, to satisfy for my sins, and to obtain the assistance of your grace so that I may persevere to the end in doing your holy will, and may love and enjoy you for ever in your glory.

God our Father, you know how weak I am. Do not leave me to myself but take me under your protection

and give me grace to act upon my holy resolutions.
Enlighten my understanding with a lively faith, raise
up my will to a firm hope, and inflame it with an
ardent charity. Strengthen my weakness, and cure the
corruption of my heart. Grant that I may overcome the
enemies of my soul, and that I may make good use of
your grace, and if it be that I should die today, grant
me the gift of final perseverance.

Heavenly Father, grant that by the guidance of the
Holy Spirit we may discern your holy will, and by the
grace of the same Spirit we may also do it, gladly and
with our whole hearts, for the glory of your Son Jesus
Christ our Lord.

Grant us, O Lord, to pass this day in gladness and
peace, without stumbling and without stain; that,
reaching the eventide victorious over all temptations,
we may praise you, the eternal God, who are blessed,
and governs all things, world without end. Amen.

Mozarabic Liturgy

O God, our Father, we thank you for waking us to see
the light of this new day. Grant that we may waste
none of its hours; soil none of its moments; neglect
none of its opportunities; fail in none of its duties. And
bring us to the evening time undefeated by any
temptation, at peace with ourselves, and with you.
This we ask for your love's sake.

William Barclay*

O God, creator of light: at the rising of your sun this
morning, let the greatest of all lights, your love, rise
like the sun within our hearts.

Armenian Apostolic Church

I pray not for wealth, I pray not for honours, I pray not
for pleasures, or even the joys of poetry. I only pray
that during all my life I may have love: that I may have
pure love to love thee.

Chaitanya, an Indian Mystic

O God, our Father, help us all through this day so to
live that we may bring help to others, credit to
ourselves and to the name we bear, and joy to those
that love us, and to you.
    Cheerful when things go wrong;
    Persevering when things are difficult;
    Serene when things are irritating.
Enable us to be;
    Helpful to those in difficulties;
    Kind to those in need;
    Sympathetic to those whose hearts are sore and
    sad.
Grant that;
    Nothing may make us lose our tempers;
    Nothing may take away our joy;
    Nothing may ruffle our peace;
    Nothing may make us bitter towards anyone.
So grant that through all this day all with whom we
work, and all those whom we meet, may see in us the
reflection of the master, whose we are, and whom we
seek to serve. This we ask for your love's sake.

William Barclay

Dear Father, take this day's life into your own keeping.
Control all my thoughts and feelings. Direct all my
energies. Instruct my mind. Sustain my will. Take my
hands and make them skilful to serve you. Take my
feet and make them swift to do your bidding. Take my
eyes and keep them fixed on your everlasting beauty.
Take my mouth and make it eloquent in testimony of

143

your love. Make this a day of obedience, a day of joy
and peace. Make this day's work a little part of the
work of the kingdom of my Lord Christ, in whose
name my prayers are said.

John Baillie

As I begin this day
become flesh again
in me, Father.
Let your timeless and everlasting love
live out this sunrise to sunset
within the possibilities,
and the impossibilities
of my own, very human life.

Help me to become
Christ to my neighbour,
food to the hungry,
health to the sick,
friend to the lonely,
freedom to the enslaved,
in all my daily living.

J. Barrie Shepherd*

God, our Father, we are exceedingly frail and
indisposed to every virtuous and gallant undertaking.
Strengthen our weakness, we beseech you, that we
may do valiantly in this spiritual war; help us against
our own negligence and cowardice, and defend us
from the treachery of our unfaithful hearts; for Jesus
Christ's sake.

Thomas à Kempis

Father in heaven, you have given us a mind to know
you, a will to serve you, and a heart to love you. Be
with us today in all that we do, so that your light may
shine out in our lives.

We pray that we may be today what you created us to
be, and may praise your name in all that we do.
We pray for your Church:
may it be a true light to all nations;
May the Spirit of your Son Jesus
guide the words and actions of all Christians today.
We pray for all who are searching for truth:
bring them your light and your love.

Give us, Lord, a humble, quiet, peaceable, patient,
tender and charitable mind, and in all our thoughts,
words and deeds a taste of the Holy Spirit. Give us,
Lord, a lively faith, a firm hope, a fervent charity, a
love of you. Take from us all lukewarmness in
meditation, dullness in prayer. Give us fervour and
delight in thinking of you and your grace, your tender
compassion towards me. The things that we pray for,
good Lord, give us grace to labour for: through Jesus
Christ our Lord.

Saint Thomas More

For the presence of God
Through every moment of this day: Be with me, Lord.
Through every day of all this week: Be with me, Lord.
Through every week of all this year: Be with me, Lord.
Through every year of all this life: Be with me, Lord.
        So that when time is past,
        By grace I may at last,
        Be with you, Lord.

God be in my head, and in my understanding,
God be in mine eyes, and in my looking,
God be in my mouth, and in my speaking,
God be in my heart, and in my thinking,
God be at my end, and at my departing.

The Book of Hours

Father, you are closer to me than my own breathing, as present and life-giving as my own heart. May each breath I take, and each heartbeat I experience deepen my awareness of your presence.

Michael Buckley

O thou
who hast given me eyes
to see the light
that fills my room,
give me the inward vision
to behold thee in this place.

O thou
who hast made me to feel
the morning wind upon my limbs,
help me to feel thy presence
as I bow in worship of thee.

Chandran Devanesen

God's presence in my World
Help me today to realise that you will be speaking to me through the events of the day, through people, through things, and through creation.

Give me ears, eyes and heart to perceive you, however veiled your presence may be.

Give me insight to see through the exterior of things to the interior truth.

Give me your Spirit of discernment.

O Lord, you know how busy I must be this day.
If I forget you, do not forget me.

Jacob Astley

Searching for God
O Lord my God,
teach my heart this day where and how to see you,
where and how to find you.

You have made me and remade me,
and you have bestowed on me
all the good things I possess,
and still I do not know you.
I have not yet done that
for which I was made.

Teach me to seek you,
for I cannot seek you
unless you teach me,
or find you
unless you show yourself to me.

Let me seek you in my desire,
Let me desire you in my seeking.
Let me find you by loving you,
Let me love you when I find you.

Saint Anselm

Trust in God's Providence
My Lord God,
I have no idea where I am going.
I do not see the road ahead of me.
I cannot know for certain where it will end.
Nor do I really know myself,
and the fact that I think that I am following
        your will does not mean that I am
        actually doing so.
But I believe that the desire to please you
        does in fact please you.
And I hope I have that desire
        in all that I am doing.

I hope that I will never do anything apart
     from that desire.
And I know that if I do this,
you will lead me by the right road though I
     may know nothing about it.
Therefore will I trust you always though I
     may seem lost and in the shadow
     of death.
I will not fear, for you are ever with me,
and you will never leave me to face my
     perils alone.

Thomas Merton

For service
Teach us, good Lord,
to serve you as you deserve,
to give and not to count the cost,
to fight and not to heed the wounds,
to toil and not to seek for rest,
to labour and not to ask for any reward,
save that of knowing that we do your will;
through Jesus Christ our Lord.

Saint Ignatius Loyola

In the service of others
Make us worthy, Lord, to serve our fellow men
throughout the world who live and die in poverty and
hunger. Give them through our hands this day their
daily bread, and by our understanding love, give
peace and joy.

Mother Teresa of Calcutta

In God's service
Lord God, whose we are and whom we serve,
help us to glorify you this day,
     in all the thoughts of our hearts,

in all the words of our lips,
   and in all the works of our hands,
as becomes those who are your servants,
through Jesus Christ our Lord.

New Every Morning

Self-offering

Take, Lord, all my liberty. Receive my memory, my
understanding, and my whole will. Whatever I have
and possess, you have given me; to you I restore it
wholly, and to your will I utterly surrender it for my
direction. Give me the love of you only, with your
grace, and I am rich enough; nor do I ask anything
besides.

Saint Ignatius Loyola

TO GOD THE SON

Lord Jesus, grant this day, to direct and sanctify, to
rule and govern our hearts and bodies, so that all our
thoughts, words and deeds may be according to your
Father's law and thus may we be saved and protected
through your mighty help.

Morning offering

O Jesus, through the most pure heart of Mary, I offer
you all the prayers, thoughts, works, and sufferings of
this day for all the intentions of your divine heart.

Grant, O Lord, that none may love thee less this day
because of me;
that never word or act of mine may turn one soul from
thee;
and ever daring, yet one other grace would I implore,
that many souls this day, because of me,
may love thee more.

Lord make me an instrument of your peace;
    where there is hatred let me sow love,
    where there is injury let me sow pardon,
    where there is doubt let me sow faith,
    where there is despair let me give hope,
    where there is darkness let me give light,
    where there is sadness let me give joy.

O divine master, grant that I may
    not try to be comforted but to comfort,
    not try to be understood but to understand,
    not try to be loved but to love.

Because it is in giving that we are received,
    it is in forgiving that we are forgiven,
    and it is in dying that we are born to eternal life.

Ascribed to Saint Francis of Assisi

Lord Jesus,
    I give you my hands to do your work.
    I give you my feet to go your way.
    I give you my eyes to see as you do.
    I give you my tongue to speak your words.
    I give you my mind that you may think in me.
    I give you my spirit that you may pray in me.

Above all,
    I give you my heart that you may love in me,
    your Father, and all mankind.
    I give you my whole self that you may grow in me,
    so that it is you, Lord Jesus,
    who live and work and pray in me.

The Grail

I hand over to your care, Lord,
    my soul and body,
    my mind and thoughts,
    my prayers and my hopes,

my health and my work,
my life and my death,
my parents and my family,
my friends and my neighbours,
my country and all men.
Today and always.

Lancelot Andrewes

O Lord Jesus Christ, who hast created me and ordered
my course and brought me hither where I am; thou
knowest what thou wouldst make me; do with me
according to thy will, with mercy.

King Henry VI

A blessing
Lord Jesus,
Bless my memory this day that it may ever recollect
        you.
Bless my understanding that it may ever think of you.
Bless my will that it may never seek or desire that
        which may be displeasing to you.
Bless my body and all its actions.
Bless my heart with all its affections.
Bless me now and at the hour of my death.
Bless me in time and in eternity, and grant that your
        most sweet blessing may be to me a pledge of
        eternal happiness.
Bless my brethren, the faithful.
Bless my dear ones.
Bless everyone I love, and everyone to whom I owe
        any gratitude, and bring me and them to rest in
        your sacred heart for ever.

In thanksgiving
Thank you Lord Jesus Christ,
for all the benefits which you have given me,
for all the pains and insults you have born for me.

O most merciful redeemer, friend and brother,
may I know you more clearly,
love you more dearly,
and follow you more nearly.
now and for ever.

Saint Richard of Chichester

For Divine Assistance
May the strength of God guide me this day, and may
his power preserve me.
May the wisdom of God instruct me; the eye of God
watch over me; the ear of God hear me; the word of
God give sweetness to my speech; the hand of God
defend me; and may I follow the way of God.

>Christ be with me, Christ before me,
>Christ be after me, Christ within me,
>Christ beneath me, Christ above me,
>Christ at my right hand, Christ at my left,
>Christ in the fort, Christ in the chariot,
>Christ in the ship
>Christ in the heart of every man who thinks of
>me,
>Christ in the mouth of every man who speaks to
>me.
>Christ in every eye that sees me.
>Christ in every ear that hears me.

Saint Patrick's Breastplate

Guide me,
teach me,
strengthen me,
till I become like a person as you would
have me be,
pure and gentle, truthful and high-minded,
brave and able, courteous and generous,
dutiful and useful.

Charles Kingsley

152

My Lord and my God,
take me from all that keeps me from you.
My Lord and my God,
grant me all that leads me to you.
My Lord and my God,
take me from myself and give me completely to you.

Nicholas of Flue

May the Lord support us all the day long, till the
shades lengthen and the evening comes, and the busy
world is hushed, and the fever of life is over, and our
work is done. Then in his mercy, may he give us a safe
lodging and a holy rest, and peace at the last. Father,
we ask this through Jesus Christ our Lord.

John Henry Newman

Have mercy upon us.
Have mercy upon our efforts, that we
Before thee, in love and in faith,
Righteousness and humility,
May follow thee, with self-denial,
Steadfastness and courage,
And meet thee in the silence.
Give us a pure heart that we may see thee,
A humble heart that we may hear thee,
A heart of love that we may serve thee,
A heart of faith that we may love thee.

Dag Hammarskjold

O Jesus, watch over me always, especially today, or I
shall betray you like Judas.

Saint Philip Neri

Living each day to the full
Lord, let me live this day
as if it were my first day,

or my last.
Let me bring to it
all the wonder and amazement of a new-born child;
the trust
that welcomes all I meet,
expects of them only the best,
and grants them the benefit
of every possible doubt;
But let me also bring
the wisdom and experience of the aged to this day;
the tenderness
that grows from years of care and gentle giving;
the hope
that has been forged through all the fires of doubt.

J. Barrie Shepherd*

Resignation
Lord Jesus, if you will that I be in darkness, may you
be blessed: if you will that I be in light may you equally
be blessed.

If you mercifully comfort me may you be blessed, and
if you will that I be afflicted may you always equally be
blessed. Keep me from all sin and I shall fear neither
death nor hell. So long as you do not cast me off for
ever, nor blot me out of the Book of Life, no tribulation
that befalls me will hurt me because in all things I place
my trust in your sacred heart.

For humility
Lord, keep me
truly humble in whatever measure
of success this day may bring.
And grant, in all things,
whether failure or success,
that I might find you,

and finding you,
find all that I can ever ask,
or hope for.

For the help of the Saints
May holy Mary, and all the saints, intercede for us this
day with the Lord that we may be helped and
protected by him who lives and reigns forever and
ever.

To Saint Joseph
Guardian of virgins, and holy father Joseph, to whose
faithful custody Christ Jesus, innocence itself, and
Mary, virgin of virgins, were committed; I ask your
prayers that I may with spotless mind, pure heart and
chaste body, ever serve Jesus and Mary all the days of
my life.

To our patron saint
O heavenly patron, whose name I rejoice to bear, pray
for me always before the throne of God; strengthen me
in my faith; confirm me in virtue; defend me in the
fight, that being conqueror over the evil one I may
deserve to obtain everlasting glory.

Prayer to our guardian angel
Angel of God, my guardian dear,
To whom his love commits me here,
Ever this day be at my side,
To light and rule, to guard and guide.

At the day's close

To the Holy Trinity
Most Holy Trinity, I commit my life, as I do this day,
now drawing to a close, to your infinite mercy, trust

and love. For my lack of faith I ask mercy of the Father, who is swift to compassion and slow to anger; for my inability to trust your providence, I seek refuge in the humanity of the Son who was obedient unto death; for my coldness in loving, I place myself in the warmth of the Holy Spirit who alone makes our lives acceptable to you. May this night's repose refresh my body and soul so that tomorrow's dawn may find me more ready to give glory to the Father, Son and Holy Spirit.

Michael Buckley

Glory to thee, my God, this night
For all the blessings of the light;
Keep me, O keep me, king of kings,
Beneath thine own almighty wings.

Forgive me, Lord, for thy dear Son,
The ill that I this day have done,
That with the world, myself, and thee,
I, ere I sleep, at peace may be.

Teach me to live, that I may dread
The grave as little as my bed;
Teach me to die, that so I may
Rise glorious at the awful day.

Praise God, from whom all blessings flow;
Praise him, all creatures here below;
Praise him above, ye heavenly host;
Praise Father, Son and Holy Ghost.

Thomas Ken

To God, the Father
Heavenly Father, at this hour which marks the end of the day, I come before you again in thankfulness to glorify your name. You have watched over me through the day and now I seek your protection throughout the

night. Send me calm rest to restore my body and soul, and strengthen my faith in you. When I arise in the morning, render me worthy to pray again to you and glorify your holy name.

Michael Buckley

In thanksgiving
Almighty and eternal God, I believe all you have revealed to your holy Church, I hope in your infinite goodness and mercy and I love you with all my heart. I thank you for all the favours which you have bestowed upon me this day; for my food and drink, my health and all my powers of body and soul; for your holy lights and inspirations, your care and protection, and for all those other graces which I do not now recall or which I have not yet grown to value as I ought. I thank you for them all, heavenly Father, through Jesus Christ, your Son, our Lord.

For renewed strength
O God, with whom there is no darkness, but the night shines as the day: keep and defend us and all your children, we beseech you, throughout the coming night. Renew our hearts with your forgiveness and our bodies with untroubled sleep, that we may wake to use more faithfully your gift of life, through Jesus Christ, our Lord. Amen.

To the Lord of all
Blessed be the Lord by day, blessed be the Lord by night; blessed be the Lord when we lie down; blessed be the Lord when we rise up. For in your hands are the souls of every living thing, and the spirits of all human flesh. Into your hands I commend my spirit; you have redeemed me, O Lord, God of truth. Our Lord in heaven, assert the unity of your name, establish your

kingdom continually, and reign over us forever and ever. Amen.

Lord, may I be wakeful at sunrise to begin a new day for you; cheerful at sunset for having done my work for you; thankful at moonrise and under starshine for the beauty of your universe. And may I add what little may be in me to add to your great world.

The Abbot of Greve

O Lord my God, thank you
    for bringing this day to a close;
Thank you for giving me rest
    in body and soul.
Your hand has been over me
    and has guarded and preserved me.
Forgive my lack of faith
    and any wrong that I have done today,
    and help me to forgive all who have wronged me.
Let me sleep in peace under your protection,
    and keep me from all the temptations of darkness.
Into your hands I commend my loved ones
    and all who dwell in this house;
I commend to you my body and soul.
O God, your holy name be praised.

Dietrich Bonhoeffer

We give thanks to you, our Father, for the life and knowledge you have imparted to us through Jesus your Son; glory be yours for ever. Even as this broken bread was scattered upon the hillside and then gathered up again, so let your Church be gathered together from the ends of the earth into your kingdom. For the kingdom, the power and the glory are yours now and for ever.

The Didache

Be present, O merciful God, and protect us through the silent hours of this night, that we who are wearied by the changes and chances of this fleeting world may repose upon your eternal changelessness, through the everlasting Christ our Lord.

Leonine Sacramentary

O Lord our God, what sins I have this day committed in word, deed, or thought, forgive me, for you are gracious, and you love all men. Grant me peaceful and undisturbed sleep, send me your guardian angel to protect and guard me from every evil, for you are the guardian of our souls and bodies, and to you we ascribe glory, to the Father and the Son and the Holy Ghost, now and for ever and unto the ages of ages.

Russian Orthodox Prayer

Into your hands, O Lord and Father, we commend our souls and our bodies, our parents and our homes, friends and servants, neighbours and kindred, our benefactors and brethren departed, all your people faithfully believing, and all who need your pity and protection. Enlighten us with your holy grace, and suffer us never more to be separated from you, who are one God in Trinity, God everlasting. Amen.

Saint Edmund of Abingdon

To God, the Son

Lord Jesus Christ, I offer you this night's repose in union with the eternal repose you have in the bosom of the Father, and the temporal repose which you had during your time on earth. I offer you every breath which I shall draw this night and every motion of my heart as so many acts of love, praise, adoration, joy, thanksgiving and homage which will be paid to you in heaven. I unite myself with your blessed mother,

Mary, Saint Joseph and all the angels and saints who will love and glorify you during this night and throughout all eternity.

Loreto Manual

Abide with us, Lord, for it is toward evening and the day is far spent; abide with us and with your whole Church. Abide with us in the evening of the day, in the evening of life, in the evening of the world. Abide with us and with all your faithful ones, O Lord, in time and eternity.

Lutheran Manual of Prayer

Watch, dear Lord with those who wake or watch or weep tonight, and give your angels charge over those who sleep. Tend your sick ones, O Lord Jesus Christ, rest your weary ones, bless your dying ones, soothe your suffering ones, shield your joyous ones, and all for your love's sake.

Saint Augustine

Show your loving kindness tonight, O Lord, to all who stand in need of your help. Be with the weak to make them strong, and with the strong to make them gentle. Cheer the lonely with your company and the worried with your peace. Prosper your Church in the fulfilment of her mighty task, and grant your blessing to all who have toiled today in Christ's name.

John Baillie

To the Holy Spirit
Holy Spirit, as the day ends and the dawn of salvation draws ever closer, we thank you for your presence which throughout the day sanctified our lives and took our fleeting moments into the bosom of the Father. We ask pardon for those lapses when through sloth and

wilfulness we forgot to live by your Spirit without which nothing is acceptable to the Father. We ask you this night for a quiet rest, and at the end your eternal peace which surpasses all understanding.

Michael Buckley

Holy Spirit, I thank you for being with me this day, for all the happiness your will has brought, and for all the toil and hardships I have had to accept. Forgive me for the times when I have forgotten you amid the cares of life. Forgive me also if I have not accepted any suffering in the same spirit as Christ my Lord. Help me to rest in peace this night, that I may wake truly refreshed and willing to spend a new day in your service. Guard me this night, as the good shepherd guards his flock. Grant that, in your mercy and love, when I close my eyes on this world for the last time, I may wake in the joy of your presence to a new everlasting day.

Harold Winstone

Holy Spirit, I thank you for the quiet moments of this busy day when you spoke to me of your abiding love. Teach me now as I lay down to rest how to listen to you when you speak in the silence of the night, in the silence of my heart. Teach me waking or sleeping how to watch and how to listen for your still, small voice which gives meaning and direction to every moment of my life.

Michael Buckley

A Blessing

For the house and family
Visit, we beseech you, O Lord, this house and family, and drive far from it all the snares of the enemy; let

your holy angels dwell therein, who will keep us in peace, and let your blessing be always upon us: through our Lord Jesus Christ.

For the less Fortunate

O God, our Father, we ask you to bless those for whom there will be no sleep tonight; those who must work throughout the night to maintain the public services, doctors who must wake to usher new life into the world, to close the eyes of those for whom this life is passing away, to ease the sufferer's pain; nurses and all who watch by the bedside of those who are ill; those who this night will not sleep because of the pain of their body or the distress of their mind; those in misfortune, who will lie down in hunger and in cold; those who are far from home and far from friends, and who are lonely as the shadows fall. Grant that in our own happiness and comfort we may never forget the sorrow and the·pain, the loneliness and the need of others in the slow, dark hours. This we ask for your love's sake.

William Barclay

General blessing

May the Lord bless us, and preserve us from all evil, and bring us to life everlasting; and may the souls of the faithful, through the mercy of God, rest in peace.

Manual of Our Lady

For a happy death

Jesus, Mary and Joseph, I give you my heart and my soul.
Jesus, Mary and Joseph, assist me in my last agony.
Jesus, Mary and Joseph may I breathe forth my soul in peace with you.

Prayer at Compline
Save us, O Lord, while waking,
and guard us while sleeping,
that when we wake, we may watch with Christ,
and when we sleep, we may rest in peace. Amen.

Roman Breviary

Nunc dimittis
At last, all powerful master, you give leave to your
servant to go in peace, according to your promise. For
my eyes have seen your salvation which you have
prepared for all nations, the light to enlighten the
Gentiles and give glory to Israel, your people. Give
praise to the Father almighty, to his Son, Jesus Christ,
the Lord, to the Spirit, who dwells in our hearts, both
now and forever. Amen.

General night prayers

*We put ourselves as far as possible in the dispositions in
which we desire to be found at the hour of death.*

O my God, I accept my death as a homage and
adoration which I owe to your divine majesty, and as a
punishment justly due to my sins; in union with the
death of my dear redeemer, and as the only means of
coming to you, my beginning and last end.

I firmly believe all the sacred truths which the Catholic
Church believes and teaches, because you have
revealed them. And by the assistance of your holy
grace, I am resolved to live and die in the communion
of your Church.

Relying upon your goodness, power, and promises, I
hope to obtain pardon of my sins, and life everlasting,
through the merits of your Son, Jesus Christ, my only

redeemer, and by the intercession of his blessed mother, and all the saints.

I love you with all my heart and soul, and desire to love you as the blessed do in heaven. I adore all the designs of your divine providence, resigning myself entirely to your will.

I also love my neighbour for your sake, as I love myself; I forgive all who have injured me, and I ask pardon of all whom I have injured.

I renounce the devil, with all his works; the world, with all its empty show; the flesh, with all its temptations.

I desire to be dissolved, and to be with Christ. Father, into your hands I commend my spirit.

Lord Jesus, receive my soul.

May the blessed virgin Mary, Saint Joseph and all the saints, pray for us to our Lord, that we may be preserved this night from sin and all evils.
Amen.

Blessed Saint Michael, defend us in the day of battle, that we may not be lost at the dreadful judgment.
Amen.

O my good angel, whom God, by his divine mercy, has appointed to be my guardian, enlighten and protect me, direct and govern me this night.
Amen.

May the almighty and merciful Lord give us pardon, absolution, and remission of our sins.
Amen.

Grant, O Lord, this night.
To keep us without sin.

Have mercy on us, O Lord.
Have mercy on us.
Let your mercy, O Lord, be upon us.
As we have hoped in you.
O Lord, hear my prayer.
And let my cry come to you.

Let us pray
Visit, we beseech you, O Lord, this house and family,
and drive far from it all the snares of the enemy; let
your holy angels dwell herein, who may keep us in
peace, and let your blessing be always upon us.
Through Christ our Lord. **Amen.**

Family Prayer

---

*The Christian family is the Church in its smallest and most
powerful form. When the family gathers together to pray then
Christ is in the midst in a special way. He blesses the father,
mother and children in their unique relationship with one
another. Through sharing in prayer the family grows
together in Christ.*

For the family: parents and children

Heavenly Father bless us all this day. In our lives at
work, at school and at home help us always to do your
holy will, and to know that in doing it we are pleasing
to you and fulfilling your plan for our salvation.

Michael Buckley

For appreciation of each other

We thank you, Father, for the gift of Jesus your Son
who came to our earth and lived in a simple home. We
have a greater appreciation of the value and dignity of
the human family because he loved and was loved
within its shelter. Bless us this day; may we grow in
love for each other in our family and so give thanks to
you who are the maker of all human families and our
abiding peace.

Michael Buckley

To the Holy Spirit

Holy Spirit, be with us throughout this day.
Strengthen us in our work, enlighten us in our study,
make us constantly aware of each other and of you, so

that we will live every moment of this day as you
would have us do.

Michael Buckley

For the family
Father, we pray for the family of all mankind that they
may acknowledge you as their creator and provider;
for the family of our nation that we may live in peace
and encourage other nations to do likewise; for the
families of this neighbourhood with whom you have
chosen us to share your presence. Finally, for our own
family that your peace may descend upon us so that
from our inner awareness of your presence we may
witness your love for the whole human family.

Michael Buckley

In gratitude
Thank you, Father, for having created us and given us
to each other in the human family.
Thank you for being with us in all our joys and
sorrows, for your comfort in our sadness, your
companionship in our loneliness.
Thank you for yesterday, today, tomorrow and for the
whole of our lives.
Thank you for friends, for health and for grace.
May we live this and every day conscious of all that
has been given to us.

Michael Buckley

For harmony
Lord Jesus Christ, be with us as a family so that we
may always have a great love for your Sacred Heart.
Make us gentle, courteous, and loving in our dealings
with each other; take from us all misunderstanding so
that no angry or bitter word may cross our lips, and

grant that always we treat each other as you treated
those with whom you shared your human family.

Michael Buckley

Family and friends
Lord Jesus Christ,
I praise and thank you for my parents and
my brothers and sisters,
whom you have given me to cherish.
Surround them with your tender, loving care,
teach them to love and serve one another
in true affection,
and to look to you in all their needs.
I place them all in your care,
knowing that your love for them is greater
than my own.
Keep us close to one another in this life
and conduct us at the last to our true
and heavenly home.
Blessed be God for ever. Amen.

For parents
Heavenly Father, from whom all parenthood comes,
teach us so to understand our children that they may
grow in your wisdom and love according to your holy
will. Fill us with sensitive respect for the great gift of
human life which you have committed to our care,
help us to listen with patience to their worries and
problems and give us the tolerance to allow them to
develop, as individuals, as your Son did under the
loving guidance of Mary and Joseph.

Michael Buckley

Father, bless the parents of this home. Help them in all
their endeavours, sustain them in their trials, give
them wisdom and strength to meet their

responsibilities and may they in their love for each other and for us find true joy, peace and fulfilment.

For fathers

Father, give me, like Joseph, a conscience sensitive to your holy will so that I may accept in my family those things which I do not understand. May I, like him, put the good of my wife and children above my own self-interest and thus bring to fulfilment the mysterious workings of your providence for our family.

Michael Buckley

For mothers

Father, lover of life and of the human family, who co-operated with me in the birth of my children, be with me now and help me in my task of raising them up as children of your kingdom. May they give you constant praise and adoration and be, to me, a never-ending source of gratitude and thanksgiving.

Michael Buckley

For children

Lord Jesus, who loved the little ones, bless the children of this family, guide and protect them through their growing years and throughout their lives. Be to them a true shepherd and suffer them not to fall away from your love and service. May they always listen to your voice, because they know you as their Lord and Saviour.

Michael Buckley

For expectant mothers

Father, may the little unborn one, that lies close to my heart, grow strong day by day until the time of his or her birth. At the hour of delivery may I not be afraid of the pains I may have to suffer but rejoice at the birth of another person destined to share with me in the human family in this world, and the world to come.

Growth in family love
Lord, a healthy sexual relationship is so important in marriage, that we want to thank you for ours. The priest, who prepared us for marriage, told us that the sacraments are a sign of your loving presence. Please help us not to forget that the sign of our sacrament, the sexual expression of our love, makes you present in our home. Please continue to enrich our lives and our family with your loving presence.

Tony Castle

Grace before meals

Bless us, O Lord, and these your gifts which we are about to receive from your bounty. Through Christ our Lord. Amen.

Grace after meals

We give you thanks, almighty God, for all your benefits (gifts), who lives and reigns, for ever and ever. Amen.

A selection of Graces

Lord Jesus be our holy guest,
Our morning prayer
Our evening rest,
And with this daily food impart
Thy love and grace to every heart.

A Grace used by President Eisenhower

Come Lord Jesus, be our guest
and bless what thou hast given us.

Old German Grace

Lord Jesus, who when you were on earth celebrated a
meal with joy, be with us now and fill us with your
spirit as we share food and fellowship together.

Michael Buckley

We thank you, Lord, not only for this food but for all
your many blessings which you shower upon us.

Bless, O Lord, this food to our use and ourselves to
your service, through Jesus Christ our Lord.

May the food which we bless in your name, O Lord,
give us the strength to serve you through Jesus Christ
our Lord.

Praise God from whom all blessings flow,
Praise him, all creatures here below,
Praise him above, angelic host,
Praise Father, Son and Holy Ghost.

Thomas Ken
(This doxology is often sung as a blessing)

Blessed be thou Lord God of the universe
who bringest forth bread from the earth
and makest glad the heart of men.

Ancient Hebrew Prayer

Be present at our table, Lord,
Be here and everywhere ador'd:
These creatures bless and grant that we
May feast in paradise with thee.

Non-Conformist Grace by John Cennick

For food in a world where many walk in hunger;
For faith in a world where many walk in fear;
For friends in a world where many walk alone,
We give you humble thanks O Lord.

A Girl Guide World Hunger Grace

Heavenly Father, bless this food, bless those who have
prepared it and give food to those who at this time go
hungry in our world.

Michael Buckley

Praying Continually

*The Spirit of the risen Christ is always at work in us.
Through him we praise, honour and adore God our loving
Father so that our minds and hearts are at rest in him. Our
prayer, like our lives, is through Jesus Christ our Lord. His
name is never far from our lips, so that our lives are a
perpetual offering of prayer to the Father.*

The Jesus Prayer

The power of the invocation lies in the holy name
itself, 'Jesus'. The name is the prayer. Phrases from the
litany of the holy name may prove a source of great
help in deepening our awareness of the presence and
power of God's Son and our Saviour.

> Lord Jesus Christ,
> Son of the living God
> Have mercy on me, a sinner.

The Litany of the Most Holy Name of Jesus

Lord, have mercy on us.
> **Lord, have mercy on us.**

Christ, have mercy on us.
> **Christ, have mercy on us.**

Lord, have mercy on us.
> **Lord, have mercy on us.**

Jesus, hear us.
> **Jesus, graciously hear us.**

God the Father of heaven,
> **have mercy on us.**

173

God the Son, redeemer of the world,
> **have mercy on us.**

God the Holy Spirit,
> **have mercy on us.**

Holy Trinity, one God,
> **have mercy on us.**

Jesus, Son of the living God,
> **have mercy on us.**

Jesus, splendour of the Father
> **have mercy on us.**

Jesus, brightness of eternal light,
> **have mercy on us.**

Jesus, king of glory,
> **have mercy on us.**

Jesus, Son of justice,
> **have mercy on us.**

Jesus, Son of the Virgin Mary,
> **have mercy on us.**

Jesus, most amiable,
> **have mercy on us.**

Jesus, most admirable,
> **have mercy on us.**

Jesus, mighty God,
> **have mercy on us.**

Jesus, father of the world to come,
> **have mercy on us.**

Jesus, angel of great counsel,
> **have mercy on us.**

Jesus most powerful,
> **have mercy on us.**

Jesus most patient,
> **have mercy on us.**

Jesus most obedient,
> **have mercy on us.**

Jesus, meek and humble of heart,
> **have mercy on us.**

Jesus, lover of purity,

have mercy on us.

Jesus, lover of us,

have mercy on us.

Jesus, author of life,

have mercy on us.

Jesus, perfection of all virtues,

have mercy on us.

Jesus, zealous lover of souls,

have mercy on us.

Jesus, our refuge,

have mercy on us.

Jesus, father of the poor,

have mercy on us.

Jesus, treasure of the faithful

have mercy on us.

Jesus, good shepherd,

have mercy on us.

Jesus, true light,

have mercy on us.

Jesus, eternal wisdom,

have mercy on us.

Jesus, infinite goodness,

have mercy on us.

Jesus, our way and our life,

have mercy on us.

Jesus, joy of angels,

have mercy on us.

Jesus, king of patriarchs,

have mercy on us.

Jesus, master of the apostles,

have mercy on us.

Jesus, teacher of the evangelists,

have mercy on us.

Jesus, strength of martyrs,

have mercy on us.

Jesus, light of confessors,

have mercy on us.

Jesus, purity of virgins,

have mercy on us.

Jesus, crown of all saints,

have mercy on us.

Be merciful unto us,

Jesus, spare us.

Be merciful unto us,

Jesus, spare us.

From all evil,

Jesus, deliver us.

From all sin,

Jesus, deliver us.

From your wrath,

Jesus, deliver us.

From the snares of the devil,

Jesus, deliver us.

From everlasting death,

Jesus, deliver us.

From our failure to follow your inspiration,

Jesus, deliver us.

Through the mystery of your holy incarnation,

Jesus, deliver us.

Through your nativity,

Jesus, deliver us.

Through your infancy,

Jesus, deliver us.

Through your most divine life,

Jesus, deliver us.

Through your labours,

Jesus, deliver us.

Through your agony and passion,

Jesus, deliver us.

Through your cross and abandonment,

Jesus, deliver us.

Through your death and burial,
Jesus, deliver us.
Through your resurrection,
Jesus, deliver us.
Through your ascension,
Jesus, deliver us.
Through your reign in heaven,
Jesus, deliver us.
Through your joys,
Jesus, deliver us.
Through your glory,
Jesus, deliver us.
Lamb of God, you take away the sins of the world,
Spare us, O Jesus.
Lamb of God, you take away the sins of the world.
Graciously hear us, O Jesus.
Lamb of God, you take away the sins of the world.
Jesus, graciously hear us.

Let us pray
Lord Jesus Christ, who has said: ask and you shall
receive; seek, and you shall find, knock, and it shall be
opened unto you; mercifully listen to our prayers and
grant us the gift of your divine mercy that we may ever
love you with our whole heart and never cease from
praising and glorifying your holy name. Give us, O
Lord, a perpetual love of your holy name; for you
never cease to be with those whom you establish in
your love. Who lives and reigns world without end.
Amen.

Aspirations or short prayers

To you be praise,
To you be glory,
To you be thanksgiving
   through endless ages, O blessed Trinity.

Holy Trinity, one God, have mercy on us.

Holy, holy, holy, Lord God of hosts:
   the heavens and the earth are full of your glory.

To the king of ages, immortal and invisible,
   to God alone be honour and glory
   for ever and ever.

Blessing and glory and wisdom and thanksgiving
   honour, might and power be unto our God
   for ever and ever.

May the most just, most high, and most lovable
   will of God be done in all things, be praised
   and worshipped forever.

My God and my all.

My God, make us to be one of mind in the truth and
   of one heart in charity.

My God, I love you.

Lord, I am my own enemy, when I see my peace apart
   from you.

Guard me as the apple of your eye.
Hide me in the shadow of your wings.

Teach me, O Lord, to do your will, for you
are my God.

Into your hands I commend my spirit.

Psalm 30

O my soul, I love the Lord that loves you
from eternity.

O God, make haste to my rescue,
Lord come to my aid!

Psalm 69

From all dangers, deliver us, O Lord.

O Lord, grant this day
to keep us without sin.

From all sin deliver us, O Lord.

Eternal Father, I offer you the precious blood of Jesus
in satisfaction for my sins and for the needs
of the Church.

Jesus, my God, I love you above all things.

O Jesus, with all my heart I cling to you.

Jesus, for love of you, with you and for you.

Praised be Jesus Christ
now and forever.

My Jesus, mercy.

My sweetest Jesus, be not my
   judge, but my Saviour.

O Jesus, be to me Jesus, and save me.

O Christ Jesus, my helper and my redeemer.

Deliver me, Lord Jesus Christ, from all my iniquities
   and from every evil, make me ever hold fast to
   your commandments and never allow me to be
   separated from you.

We adore you, O Christ, and we bless you;
   because by your holy cross you have redeemed
   the world.

Sacred Heart of Jesus, protect our families.

Heart of Jesus, burning with love for us,
   inflame our hearts with love for you.

Sweet Heart of Jesus,
   grant that I may love you more.

Heart of Jesus, I place all my trust in you.

Jesus, meek and humble of heart,
   make my heart like unto yours.

O Heart of love, I put all my trust in you;
   for I fear all things from my own weakness,
   but I hope for all things from your goodness.

Most Sacred Heart of Jesus,
   have mercy on us.

O sweetest Heart of Jesus I implore,
   that I may ever love you more and more.

May the Sacred Heart of Jesus be everywhere loved.

Sacred Heart of Jesus, I believe in your love for me.

All for you, most sacred heart of Jesus, all for you.

Sweet Heart of Jesus, be my love.

Sacred Heart of Jesus, let me love you and make
   you loved.

May the most holy and most divine sacrament be
   every moment praised and adored.

Blessed be the holy and immaculate conception of
   the most Blessed Virgin Mary, mother of God.

Mary, mother of God and mother of mercy, pray for
   me and for the departed.

O Mary, conceived without sin, pray for us
   who have recourse to you.

Pray for us, O holy mother of God, that we may be
   made worthy of the promises of Christ.

O Mary, make me live in God, with God, and for God.

Draw me after you, holy mother.

O Mary, may your children persevere in loving you.

Special Occasions

No situation is outside the light of the resurrection, the power of the Holy Spirit or God the Father's love. Every aspect of our lives is under this powerful influence. When we pray, whether it be for the needs of the world, or our own spiritual growth, then God is there to meet our every desire. If we ask for bread he will not give us a stone.

Prayers from the Roman Missal

For the universal Church
God, our Father,
by the promise you made
in the life, death and resurrection of Christ your Son,
you bring together in your Spirit, from all the nations,
a people to be your own.
Keep the Church faithful to its mission:
may it be a leaven in the world
renewing us in Christ,
and transforming us into your family.

For the local Church
God our Father,
in all the churches scattered throughout the world
you show forth the one, holy, Catholic and apostolic
    Church.
Through the gospel and the eucharist
bring your people together in the Holy Spirit
and guide us in your love.
Make us a sign of your love for all people,
and help us to show forth
the living presence of Christ in the world.

For the election of pope or bishop
Lord God,
you are our eternal shepherd and guide.
In your mercy grant your Church a shepherd
who will walk in your ways
and whose watchful care will bring us your blessing.

For the Pope
Lord,
source of eternal life and truth,
give to your shepherd N.
a spirit of courage and right judgment,
a spirit of knowledge and love.
By governing with fidelity those entrusted to his care
may he, as successor to the apostle Peter
    and Vicar of Christ,
build your Church into a sacrament of unity, love, and
    peace for all the world.

For the Bishop
God, eternal shepherd,
you tend your Church in many ways,
and rule us with love.
Help your chosen servant N.
as pastor for Christ,
to watch over your flock.
Help him to be a faithful teacher,
a wise administrator, and a holy priest.

For a Council or Synod
Lord,
protector and ruler of your Church,
fill your servants with a spirit of understanding, truth
    and peace.
Help them to strive with all their hearts
to learn what is pleasing to you,
and to follow it with all their strength.

For priests
Father,
you have appointed your Son Jesus Christ eternal high
  priest.
Guide those he has chosen to be ministers of word and
  sacrament
and help them to be faithful
in fulfilling the ministry they have received.

For the priest himself
Father,
unworthy as I am, you have chosen me
to share in the eternal priesthood of Christ
and the ministry of your Church.
May I be an ardent but gentle servant
of your gospel and your sacraments.

For the ministers of the Church
Father,
you have taught the ministers of your Church
not to desire that they be served but to serve their
  brothers and sisters.
May they be effective in their work
and persevering in their prayer,
performing their ministry with gentleness and concern
  for others.

For Priestly vocations
Father,
in your plan for our salvation you provide shepherds
  for your people,
Fill your Church with the spirit of courage and love.
Raise up worthy ministers for your altars
and ardent but gentle servants of the gospel.

For Religious
Father,
you inspire and bring to fulfilment every good
   intention.
Guide your people in the way of salvation
and watch over those who have left all things
to give themselves entirely to you.
By following Christ and renouncing worldly power
   and profit,
may they serve you and their brothers faithfully
in the spirit of poverty and humility.

For Religious vocations
Father,
you call all who believe in you to grow perfect in love
by following in the footsteps of Christ your Son.
May those whom you have chosen to serve you as
   religious
provide by their way of life
a convincing sign of your kingdom
for the Church and the whole world.

For the Laity
God our Father,
you send the power of the gospel into the world
as a life-giving leaven.
Fill with the Spirit of Christ
those whom you call to live in the midst of the
world and its concerns;
help them by their work on earth
to build up your eternal kingdom.

For the Unity of Christians
Lord,
hear the prayers of your people

and bring the hearts of believers together in your
    praise
and in common sorrow for their sins.
Heal all divisions among Christians
that we may rejoice in the perfect unity of your Church
and move together as one
to eternal life in your kingdom.

For the spread of the Gospel
God our Father,
you will all men to be saved
and come to the knowledge of your truth.
Send workers into your great harvest
that the gospel may be preached to every creature
and your people, gathered together by the word of life
and strengthened by the power of the sacraments,
may advance in the way of salvation and love.

For pastoral and spiritual meetings
Lord,
pour out on us the spirit of understanding,
    truth and peace.
Help us to strive with all our hearts
to know what is pleasing to you,
and when we know your will
make us determined to do it.

For the nation (state)
God our Father,
you guide everything in wisdom and love.
Accept the prayers we offer for our nation;
by the wisdom of our leaders and integrity of our
    citizens,
may harmony and justice be secured
and may there be lasting prosperity and peace.

For those who serve in public office
Almighty and eternal God,
you know the longings of men's hearts
and you protect their rights.
In your goodness,
watch over those in authority,
so that people everywhere may enjoy
freedom, security, and peace.

For the assembly of national leaders
Father,
you guide and govern everything with order and love.
Look upon the assembly of our national leaders
and fill them with the spirit of your wisdom.
May they always act in accordance with your will
and their decisions be for the peace
    and well-being of all.

For the king/queen or head of state
God our Father,
all earthly powers must serve you.
Help your servant N. (our King/Queen/President)
to fulfil his/her responsibilities worthily and well.
By honouring and striving to please you at all times,
may he/she secure peace and freedom
for the people entrusted to him/her.

For peace and justice
God our Father,
you reveal that those who work for peace
will be called your sons.
Help us to work without ceasing
for that justice
which brings true and lasting peace.

For peace
God of perfect peace,
violence and cruelty can have no part with you.
May those who are at peace with one another
hold fast to the good will that unites them;
may those who are enemies forget their hatred
and be healed.

In time of war and civil disturbance
God our Father,
maker and lover of peace,
to know you is to live,
and to serve you is to reign.
All our faith is in your saving help;
protect us from men of violence
and keep us safe from weapons of hate.

At the New Year
Almighty God,
with you there is no beginning and no end
for you are the origin and goal of all creation.
May this new year which we dedicate to you
bring us abundant prosperity and growth in holy
    living.

For the progress of peoples
Father,
You have given all peoples one common origin,
and your will is to gather them as one family in
    yourself.
Fill the hearts of all men with the fire of your love
and the desire to ensure justice for all their brothers
    and sisters.
By sharing the good things you gave us
may we secure justice and equality for every human
    being,

an end to all division,
and a human society built on love and peace.

For the blessing of man's labour
God our Father,
by the labour of man you govern and guide to
    perfection
the work of creation.
Hear the prayers of your people
and give all men work that enhances their human
    dignity
and draws them closer to each other
in the service of their brothers.

For productive land
God our Father,
we acknowledge you as the only source of growth and
    abundance.
With your help we plant our crops
and by your power they produce our harvest.
In your kindness and love
make up for what is lacking in our efforts.

After the harvest
Father, God of goodness
you give man the land to provide him with food.
May the produce we harvest sustain our lives,
and may we always use it for your glory and the good
    of all.

For those who suffer from famine
All-powerful Father,
God of goodness,
you provide for all your creation.
Give us an effective love for our brothers and sisters
who suffer from lack of food.

Help us do all we can to relieve their hunger,
that they may serve you with carefree hearts.

For refugees
Lord,
no one is a stranger to you
and no one is ever far from your loving care.
In your kindness watch over refugees and exiles,
those separated from their loved ones,
young people who are lost,
and those who have left or run away from home.
Bring them back safely to the place where they long
to be, and help us always to show your kindness
to strangers and those in need.

For those unjustly deprived of liberty
Father,
your Son came among us as a slave
to free the human race from the bondage of sin.
Rescue those unjustly deprived of liberty,
and restore them to the freedom you wish for all men
as your sons.

For persecuted Christians
Father,
in your mysterious providence,
your Church must share in the sufferings of Christ
    your Son.
Give the spirit of patience and love
to those who are persecuted for their faith in you
that they may always be true and faithful witnesses
to your promise of eternal life.

For prisoners
Father of mercy,
the secrets of all hearts are known to you alone.

You know who is just and you forgive the unjust.
Hear our prayers for those in prison.
Give them patience and hope in their sufferings,
and bring them home again soon.

For the sick
Father,
your Son accepted our sufferings
to teach us the virtue of patience in human illness.
Hear the prayers we offer for our sick brothers and
    sisters.
May all who suffer pain, illness or disease
realise that they are chosen to be saints,
and know that they are joined to Christ
in his suffering for the salvation of the world.

For the dying
God of power and mercy,
you have made death itself
the gateway to eternal life.
Look with love on our dying brother (sister),
and make him (her) one with your Son in his suffering
    and death,
that, sealed with the blood of Christ,
he (she) may come before you free from sin.

For a happy death
Father,
you made us in your own image
and your Son accepted death for our salvation.
Help us to keep watch in prayer at all times.
May we be free from sin when we leave this world
and rejoice in peace with you for ever.

In time of earthquake
God our Father,
you set the earth on its foundation.

Keep us safe from the danger of earthquakes
and let us always feel the presence of your love.
May we be secure in your protection
and serve you with grateful hearts.

For rain
Lord God,
in you we live and move and have our being.
Help us in our present time of trouble,
send us the rain we need,
and teach us to seek your lasting help
on the way to eternal life.

For fine weather
All-powerful and ever-living God,
we find security in your forgiveness.
Give us the fine weather we pray for so that we may
    rejoice in your gifts of kindness,
and use them always for your glory and our good.

To avert storms
Father,
all the elements of nature obey your command.
Calm the storms that threaten us,
and turn our fear of your power
into praise of your goodness.

For any need
God our Father,
our strength in adversity,
our health in weakness,
our comfort in sorrow,
be merciful to your people.
As you have given us the punishment we deserve,
give us also new life and hope as we rest in your
    kindness.

For forgiveness of sins
Lord,
hear the prayers of those who call on you,
forgive the sins of those who confess to you,
and in your merciful love
give us your pardon and your peace.

For charity
Lord,
fill our hearts with the spirit of your charity,
that we may please you by our thoughts,
and love you in our brothers and sisters.

For promoting harmony
God our Father,
source of unity and love,
make your faithful people one in heart and mind
that your Church may live in harmony,
be steadfast in its profession of faith,
and secure in unity.

For the family
Father,
we look to your loving guidance and order
as the pattern of all family life.
By following the example of the holy family of your
    Son,
in mutual love and respect,
may we come to the joy of our home in heaven.

For relatives and friends
Father,
by the power of your Spirit
you have filled the hearts of your faithful people
with gifts of love for one another.
Hear the prayers we offer for our relatives and friends.

Give them health of mind and body
that they may do your will with perfect love.

For our oppressors
Father,
according to your law of love
we wish to love sincerely all who oppress us.
Help us to follow the commandments of your new
    covenant,
that by returning good for the evil done to us,
we may learn to bear the ill-will of others out of love
    for you.

Prayers from other sources

For the Church
Think of your Church, O Lord. Free it from all evil and
make it perfect in your love. Make your people holy,
and lead them to the kingdom you have prepared for
them. For yours is the power and the glory for all
eternity.

Early Christian Prayer

Almighty and everlasting God, who hast revealed thy
glory in Christ among the nations: Preserve the works
of thy mercy, that thy Church which is spread
throughout the world may persevere with steadfast
faith and love in the confession of thy name, through
Jesus Christ our Lord.

Gelasian Sacramentary

God, your Son left his Church as a memorial of his
presence and as a witness of his divine mission. May
all Christians grow in the exercise of faith, hope and
love that her life will be so renewed that she, who is
the light of the world, may shine brightly before
everyone.

For the local church or parish

O God, the creator, redeemer and sanctifier of all who believe and trust in you, bless the Church in this place in its work for the furtherance of your kingdom on earth. Strengthen the faith and commitment of its members; deepen the bonds of community and grant to all a spirit of sharing, generosity and self-sacrifice.

Michael Buckley

For the Pope

O almighty and eternal God, have mercy on your servant, our Pope, and direct him into the way of everlasting salvation. May he desire by your grace those things that are agreeable to you, and perform them with all his strength. Through Christ our Lord. Amen.

O God, shepherd and ruler of all the faithful, look favourably on your servant *N.* whom you have made chief pastor of your Church. May his words and example profit those over whom he is placed, so that he and his flock may together attain everlasting life.

For Priests

Lord Jesus, bless all priests and give them grace to do your great work on earth. Keep them, Lord, close to your heart and under the shadow of your protection. Bless their labours for you and grant that their harvest of souls may be a source of joy and consolation to them during life and may merit an everlasting reward for them in death, that having led many souls to you they may see you face to face.

For Vocations

Lord Jesus Christ, shepherd of souls, who called the apostles to be fishers of men, raise up new apostles in

your holy Church. Teach them that to serve you is to
reign: to possess you is to possess all things. Kindle in
the young hearts of our sons and daughters the fire of
zeal for souls. Make them eager to spread your
kingdom upon earth. Grant them courage to follow
you, who are the way, the truth and the life; who lives
and reigns for ever and ever. Amen.

A Simple Prayer Book

For Christian Discipleship
Lord our God, you have given your Son to the world
and in his Church he nourishes his faithful with the
gospel and the sacraments. We ask you that Christians
everywhere may find strength to tread his path; and
that they be for each other and with each other so that
the power of your grace may shine through their lives.
Through Christ our Lord.

For Christian Unity
*Father, may they be one in us, as you are in me, and I am in
you, so that the world may believe it was you who sent me.*
John 17:21.

Let us pray

O God of Peace, who through your son Jesus Christ
did proclaim one faith for the salvation of mankind,
send your grace and blessing on all Christians who are
striving to draw nearer to you and to each other. Give
us boldness to seek only your glory and the
advancement of your kingdom. Unite us all in you,
Father, who with your Son and the Holy Spirit, are one
God, for ever and ever.

O God, you bring back to the right way those who
have gone astray, you gather the scattered, and keep

together those you have gathered. Mercifully fill
Christian people with the grace of your own oneness,
that they may reject all division and, being one in
communion with the true shepherd of your Church,
be able to serve you as you should be served.

For the Missions

You desire, O God, that all men should come to know
truth and all be saved. Send then, we pray, workers
into your harvest field, and give them power boldly to
proclaim your word. Thus may your gospel be
received and honoured throughout the world, and
every people know you, the one true God, and your
Son whom you have sent, our Lord Jesus Christ.

For the Spread of the Gospel

Almighty God, from whom all thoughts of truth and
peace proceed. Kindle, we pray thee, in the hearts of
all men the true love of peace, and guide with thy
pure and peaceable wisdom those who take counsel
for the nations of the earth; that in tranquillity thy
kingdom may go forward, till the earth is filled with
the knowledge of thy love; through Jesus Christ our
Lord. Amen.

Lord, your love and salvation was meant for everyone,
and Christians are your missionaries. Because you
have made Christians one in Christ, so those who
believe and are baptised have brothers and sisters all
over the world, in Africa, Asia, America, Australia and
Europe. Grant that this life of Christ may grow
stronger, drawing them ever closer together in love
and unity and helping them to become more zealous
for the spread of the gospel.

For the enlightenment of the Nations

Almighty God, who led the wise men by the light of a star to your infant Son to worship in him the glory of the Word made flesh: guide by your truth the nations of the earth that imitating the wise men the whole world may find your Son.

A Christian's Prayer Book

For patriotism

Heavenly Father, purify in all the people of this land, their love for the nation according to the mind of your Son Jesus Christ, who knew what was good for the peace of his land and people. May everyone strive by word and action to foster peace among the people of all social classes and creeds, so that, living in harmony and justice, they may be a Christian light to other nations, such as your Son would have them be.

Michael Buckley

For Remembrance Sunday

Heavenly Father, we remember before you, with gratitude, those who gave their lives for the cause of our nation. Because you have taken them to yourself they shall not grow old as we that are left grow old. Age shall not weary them, nor the years condemn. Grant that their sacrifice may bear fruit in the Christian quality of our lives and all those who share with them a common fatherland.

Laurence Binyon*

For Peace and Justice

Almighty and eternal God,
may your grace enkindle in all of us a love for the many unfortunate people whom poverty and misery reduce to a condition of life unworthy of human beings. Arouse in the hearts of those who call you Father a hunger and thirst for justice and peace, and

for fraternal charity in deeds and in truth. Grant, O Lord, peace in our days, peace to souls, peace to families, peace to our country, and peace among nations.

Pope Pius XII

For Social Justice and Peace
Jesus, Son of God, friend of all social classes, grant that the rich may so evaluate their wealth that they may generously follow the simplicity of your dedicated life, and so help the poor to lead a life worthy of their human dignity. Grant that all may see themselves as your brothers and sisters who became poor for our sake.

Michael Buckley

For Industrial Peace
Father, your love taught us that we are members of one family; grant that all employers and employees, conscious of their mutual rights and obligations, may avoid bitterness and distrust in industrial disputes and work together for the good of our nation and people.

Michael Buckley

General Intercession for Peace
In peace, let us beseech the Lord
for the peace that is from above
and the salvation of our souls;
for the peace of the whole world
and of the holy churches of God
and of all men.
For our homes, that they may be holy,
and for all our pastors, teachers and governors;
for our city (township, village) and country
and all who dwell therein;
for all that travel by land, by air, by water;

for the sick and all who need your pity and protection.
On all, have mercy, and preserve all, O God, by your
grace:
for to you, O Lord, is due glory, honour, and worship;
world without end.

Liturgy of Saint John Chrysostom

For the unemployed
Heavenly Father, who wills that every individual
should belong to the human community, look with
compassion on those who suffer distress through lack
of work; take from them the feeling of rejection. Grant
that they be set free from want and insecurity and may
they soon find employment, as those in the gospel
story who were called at the eleventh hour to labour in
the vineyard, through Jesus Christ, our Lord. Amen.

Michael Buckley

For work
God our Father,
through and by the work of our hands
your mighty work of creation continues.
Hear the prayers of your people
and give all who seek employment
the opportunity to enhance their human dignity
and draw closer to one another
in mutual interdependence.

Tony Castle

For the homeless
Have mercy, O Lord our God, on those whom war or
oppression or famine have robbed of homes and
friends, and aid all those who try to help them. We
commend also into your care those whose homes are
broken by conflict and lack of love; grant that where

the love of man has failed, the divine compassion may
heal; through Jesus Christ our Lord.

For immigrants
Father, conscious that your Son, while still an infant,
made his home in a foreign land, we pray for all those
from other countries who now live among us. May
their customs and culture be appreciated and may they
be offered true Christian friendship and
understanding as a token of gratitude for that welcome
which was once offered to your only Son.

Michael Buckley

For the Persecuted Church
Mercifully hear the prayers of your Church, Lord, that
all hostility and falsehood may be brought to nothing,
and that she may serve you in untroubled freedom.

For the sick
Almighty and ever-living God, physician who brings
eternal healing to those who believe, hear us as we ask
your compassionate help for your servant *N*. who is
sick. Give him/her back good health, and enable
him/her to return thanks to you in the assembly of the
faithful.

For a happy death
Almighty and merciful God, mankind receives from
you the means of salvation and the grace to attain
everlasting life. Look kindly on all your servants and
fortify the souls you have created, so that when the
hour of departure comes they may be free from sin and
fit to be brought by the holy angels to you in your
glory.

For those suffering from an incurable disease
Father, lover of life, we pray for those suffering from
disease for which, at present, there is no known cure;
give them confidence in your love and never-failing
support and a stronger faith in the resurrection. Grant
wisdom and perseverance to all working to discover
the causes of the disease, so that they see in their
labours the ministry of your Son, who himself showed
forth his divine power by healing those who came to
him.

George Appleton

For those who mourn
Lord Jesus Christ, you wept over the death of Lazarus
and said *Blessed are those who mourn*. Visit, we beseech
you, with your compassion the homes and hearts of
those who mourn the loss of their loved one and may
their hope in the resurrection sustain them in this hour
of trial.

For the distressed
God, whose mercy and compassion never fail, look
kindly upon the sufferings of all mankind: the needs of
the homeless; the anxieties of prisoners; the pains of
the sick and the injured; the sorrows of the bereaved;
the helplessness of the aged and weak. Comfort and
strengthen them for the sake of your Son, our Saviour
Jesus Christ.

Saint Anselm

For the aged
Lord Jesus Christ, who heard the prayers of your two
disciples at Emmaus and stayed with them at eventide,
stay we pray you, with all your people in the evening
of their life. Make yourself known to them, and let
your light shine upon their path; and whenever they

shall pass through the valley of the shadow of death, be with them to the end.

George Appleton

For writers, artists, broadcasters
Almighty God, who has proclaimed your eternal truth by the voice of the prophets and evangelists: direct and bless, we ask you, those who, in this our generation, speak where many listen and write what many read; that they may do their part in making the heart of the people wise, its mind sound, and its will righteous; to the honour of Jesus Christ our Lord.

The Boys' Prayer Book

For students
Grant, Lord, to all students, to love and know that which is worth loving and knowing, to praise that which pleases you most, to esteem that which is most precious to you, and to dislike whatsoever is evil in your eyes.

Thomas à Kempis

For those on a journey or pilgrimage
Hear our prayers, Lord, and give your servants a safe and happy journey; and may your help be with them in all the changes and chances of their way through this life.

For those at sea
You, O God, brought our spiritual forefathers through the Red Sea, leading them by deep waters while they sang praises to your name. We beg you to watch over your servants who are aboard ship, give them a good passage, and bring them safely to harbour.

For those who travel by air

O God, protector of those who trust in your power,
send a good angel from heaven to go with travellers
through the air, that they may be watched over in their
journeyings and brought safely to their destination.

O Almighty God, who makest the clouds thy chariots,
and walkest upon the wings of the wind: we beseech
thee for all who travel by air to their several duties and
destinations; that thy presence may ever be with them,
to pilot, to speed, and to protect; through Jesus Christ
our Lord.

Eric Milner-White

For motorists

Almighty God, ever active and ever at rest, give us a
mind so set at peace with you that we may use our
vehicles with a true spirit of courtesy and respect for
others so that, avoiding all unnecessary tension,
anxiety and desire for speed, we may protect others
and ourselves from needless danger and distress and
come to our destination safely and in your grace.

Michael Buckley

Protect us, O Lord, from all danger to men that may
arise from the difficulties of travelling, the weariness of
the body or from inconsiderate speed, and as, O Lord,
you graciously sent the archangel Raphael to be a
travelling companion and protector to the young
Tobias, so save all your children from all perils of soul
and body, so that, journeying along the ways of this
world in your sight, they may deserve to reach the
haven of eternal salvation. Through Christ our Lord.

Pope John XXIII

For those dear to us

O God, by the grace of the Holy Spirit, you have filled
the hearts of your faithful Christians with gifts of love.
Grant health of mind and body to your servants, the
men and women for whom we beseech your kindness:
may they love you with all their strength and do your
will with all their heart.

For absent loved ones

Almighty Father, you watch over with love the affairs
of all your children, mercifully hear our prayers for
those whom we love and from whom we are now
parted. Be with them, Lord, and protect them in all the
trials of this life. Teach us, and them, to feel and know
that you are always near, and that we are never parted
from each other if we are united in you through Jesus
Christ our Lord.

Michael Buckley

For true Christian homes

Lord Jesus, who grew up in an earthly home obedient
to earthly parents, bless all the homes in this parish.
May the parents impart to their children the
knowledge of you and your love, and may the children
love, obey and succour their parents; and bring us all
to the joy of your heavenly home, for your great
name's sake.

For the intercession of the Saints

Keep us safe, Lord, from every danger which
threatens mind or body. In your goodness give peace
and security, asked for us by the prayers of the blessed
and glorious ever-virgin Mary, mother of God, of
blessed Joseph, of your blessed apostles Peter and
Paul, of blessed N. and of all the saints; so that all

hostility and falsehood may be brought to nothing,
and your Church may serve you in untroubled
freedom.

O God, our refuge and our strength, source of all
sincerity, listen to the sincere prayers of your Church:
grant that what we ask for in faith we may effectively
receive.

Prayers for spiritual growth

Knowing and loving God
My God, I love thee: not because
I hope for heaven thereby,
nor yet because who love thee not
are lost eternally.

Thou, O my Jesus, thou didst me
upon the cross embrace;
for me didst bear the nails and spear
and manifold disgrace.

And griefs and torments numberless
and sweat of agony;
even death itself – and all for one
who was thine enemy.

Then why, O blessed Jesu Christ,
should I not love thee well;
not for the sake of winning heaven
or of escaping hell;
not with the hope of gaining aught,
nor seeking a reward:
but as thyself has loved me,
O ever-loving Lord!

Even so I love thee, and will love
and in thy praise will sing,
solely because thou art my God
and my eternal king.

Saint Francis Xavier

O Lord, my God, my only hope, hear me, lest through
weariness I should not wish to seek you, but may
ardently seek your face evermore. Give me the
strength to seek, you who have caused me to find you,
and have given me the hope of finding you more and
more.

Saint Augustine

God, our Father, we find it difficult to come to you,
    because our knowledge of you is so imperfect.

In our ignorance we have imagined you to be our
enemy;
    we have wrongly thought that you take pleasure in
    punishing our sins;
    and we have foolishly conceived you to be a tyrant
    over human life.

But since Jesus came among us,
    he has shown that you are loving,
    that you are on our side against all that stunts life,
    and that our resentment against you was
    groundless.

So we come to you, asking you to forgive our past
ignorance,
    and wanting to know more and more of you and
    your forgiving love, through Jesus Christ our Lord.

Late have I loved you, O beauty so ancient and so new;
    late have I loved you.

For behold you were within me, and I outside;
　　and I sought you outside and in my ugliness fell
　　upon those lovely things that you have made.
You were with me and I was not with you.
I was kept from you by those things,
　　yet had they not been in you, they would not have
　　been at all.
You called and cried to me and broke upon my
deafness;
　　and you sent forth your light and shone upon me,
　　and chased away my blindness;
You breathed fragrance upon me,
　　and I drew in my breath and do not pant for you:
I tasted you and I now hunger and thirst for you;
　　you touched me, and I have burned for your peace.

Saint Augustine

Give me, O Lord, a steadfast heart which no unworthy
thought can drag downwards; an unconquered heart
which no tribulation can wear out; an upright heart
which no unworthy purpose may tempt aside. Bestow
upon me also, O Lord my God, understanding to
know thee, diligence to seek thee, wisdom to find
thee, and a faithfulness that may finally embrace thee;
through Jesus Christ, our Lord.

Saint Thomas Aquinas

Lord, where shall I find you?
High and hidden is your place.
And where shall I not find you?
The world is full of your glory.

I have sought your nearness,
With all my heart I called you
and in going out to meet you
I found you coming in to meet me.

Judah Halebi

O my God, give me thy grace so that the things of this earth and things more naturally pleasing to me, may not be as close as thou art to me. Keep thou my eyes, my ears, my heart from clinging to the things of this world. Break my bonds, raise my heart. Keep my whole being fixed on thee. Let me never lose sight of thee; and while I gaze on thee, let my love of thee grow more and more every day.

John Henry Newman

Love of God

You who are love itself give me the grace of love, give me yourself, so that all my days may finally empty into the one day of your eternal life.

Karl Rahner

O God, who by love alone are great and glorious, who are present and live with us by love alone: grant us likewise by love to attain another self, by love to live in others, and by love to come to our glory to see and accompany your love throughout all eternity.

Thomas Traherne

Come, Lord, work upon us, set us on fire and clasp us close, be fragrant to us, draw us to your loveliness, let us love, let us run to you.

Saint Augustine

Lord, make me like crystal that your light
may shine through me.

Katherine Mansfield

Lord, enfold me in the depths of your heart; and there hold me, refine, purge and set me on fire; raise me aloft until my own self knows utter annihilation.

Teilhard de Chardin

O Lord God, give me true charity which never fails so that my life may shine as a light which warms my own heart and gives comfort to others.

Saint Columbanus

O God, reign over us in spite of our infidelities; may the fire of your love quench every other fire. What can we see that is lovable outside of you, and which we do not find perfectly in you, who are the source of all good? Grant us the grace of loving you; we shall then love you only, and we shall love you eternally.

François Fénelon

O God, worthy of an infinite love, I have nothing which can adequately measure thy dignity but such is my desire towards thee, that if I had all that thou hast, I would gladly and thankfully resign all to thee.

Saint Gertrude

Teach us, O Lord, to fear without being afraid; to fear thee in love that we may love thee without fear; through Jesus Christ our Lord.

Christina Rossetti

O my God, let me walk in the way of love which knoweth not how to seek self in anything whatsoever. Let me love thee for thyself, and nothing else but in and for thee. Let me love nothing instead of thee, for to give all for love is a most sweet bargain. Let thy love work in me and by me, and let me love thee as thou wouldst be loved by me.

Dame Gertrude More

For self-knowledge
Lord Jesus, let me know myself; let me know thee,
And desire nothing else but thee.

Let me love myself only if I love thee,
And do all things for thy sake.
Let me humble myself and exalt thee,
And think of nothing else but thee.
Let me die to myself and live in thee,
And take whatever happens as coming from thee.
Let me forsake myself and walk after thee,
And ever desire to follow thee.
Let me flee from myself and turn to thee,
That so I may merit to be defended by thee.
Let me fear for myself, let me fear thee,
And be among those that are chosen by thee.
Let me distrust myself and trust in thee,
And ever obey for the love of thee.
Let me cleave to nothing but thee,
And ever be poor because of thee.
Look upon me that I may love thee,
Call me, that I may see thee,
And forever possess thee, for all eternity.

Saint Augustine

I thank thee, Lord, for knowing me better than I know myself, and for letting me know myself better than others know me. Make me, I pray, better than they suppose, and forgive me for what they do not know. Lord Jesus, eternal word of the Father, who brought us the words of the gospel, grant me through them, to know you and to know myself. Show me my wretchedness and your mercy; my sin and your grace; my poverty and your riches; my weakness and your strength; my stupidity and your wisdom; my darkness and your light.

The spirit of true prayer

O Lord God, who never failest both to hear and to answer the prayer that is sincere: let not our hearts be upon the world when our hands are lifted up to pray, nor our prayers end upon our lips, but go forth with power to work thy will in the world; through Jesus Christ our Lord.

O God of love, who biddest thy children pray, not that thou needest to be entreated, but that we may be more capable of blessings by desiring them: make us both to desire and to entreat according to thy will, that we may receive according to thine immeasurable bounty; through Jesus Christ our Lord.

O Lord God, that art a hearer not of the voice but of the heart: make our prayer which goeth up to thee as eager as thy pity which poureth down upon us; for Christ's sake.

Dame Gertrude More

A spirit of thanksgiving

God, whose mercy is boundless and whose gifts are without end, help us always to thank you for everything that your loving power has bestowed on us. Make us realise that our desire to thank you is itself your gift and that our thankfulness is never-ending because your love is never-failing.

Michael Buckley

Courage

This is my prayer to thee, my Lord – strike, strike at the penury in my heart. Give me the strength never to disown the poor or bend my knees before insolent might, and give me the strength to surrender my strength to thy will with love.

Rabindranath Tagore

Give me, O Christ, the courage of faith. Pierce the hidden depths of my spirit like a two-edged sword. Give me your clear light to guide my conscience. Give me that love which delights me in the seclusion of my timid heart and without which I cannot know you as the Lord of all things, of atoms and stars, of human bodies and spiritual worlds. Then shall I be truly blessed in you, then shall I have my heart's desire and the purpose of my existence.

Hugo Rahner

From the cowardice that dare not face new truth,
From the laziness that is contented with half truth,
From the arrogance that thinks it knows all truth,
Good Lord, deliver me.

Prayer from Kenya

May he give us all the courage that we need to go the way he shepherds us, that when he calls we may go unfrightened. If he bids us come to him across the waters, that unfrightened we may go. And if he bids us climb the hill, may we not notice that it is a hill, mindful only of the happiness of his company. He made us for himself, that we should travel with him and see him at last in his unveiled beauty in the abiding city, where he is light and happiness and endless home.

Bede Jarrett

Serenity
God grant me
the serenity to accept the things I cannot change,
the courage to change the things I can,
and the wisdom to distinguish the one from the other.

Reinhold Niebuhr

O God, source of holy desires, right counsels and just actions, grant to your servants that peace which the world cannot give, so that our hearts may be wholly devoted to your service, and all our days, freed from dread of our enemies, may be passed in quietness under your protection.

Almighty God, you know our necessities before we ask, and our ignorance in asking, set us free from all anxious thoughts for the morrow; give us contentment with your good gifts, and confirm our faith that as we seek your kingdom, you will not suffer us to lack anything we need through Jesus Christ our Lord.

God, our Father, I turn to you in my unrest because I cannot see any way out of the present situation which troubles my spirit. In my confusion I turn to you for help and guidance because you alone can help me and nothing is impossible to you. Light up my life with faith, strengthen me in hope and fill me with love, so that I may rest in your providence which alone knows what is for my peace.

Michael Buckley

For inner silence
O Christ, my Lord, I pray that you will turn my heart to you in the depths of my being, where with the noise of creatures silenced and the clamour of bothersome thoughts stilled, I shall stay with you where I find you always present.

Father Lessius

Slowing down
Slow me down Lord,
ease the pounding of my heart
by the quieting of my mind.

Teach me the art of slowing down,
to look at a flower,
to chat to a friend,
to read a few lines from a good book.

Remind me each day of the fable
of the hare and the tortoise,
that I may know that the race
is not always to the swift,
that there is more to life than
increasing its speed.

Let me look upward into the
branches of the towering oak
and know that it grew great and
strong because it grew slowly
and well.

Slow me down, Lord, and inspire
me to send my roots deep into
the soil of life's enduring
values that I may grow toward
the stars of my greater destiny.

In time of trial

Lord Jesus, in times of trial and temptation, be my
strength and consolation. Teach me not to fear the
darkness, but rather draw me to your light. For it can
only be in darkness that you will become my light and
in your light that I may bring the light of healing love
to all I meet.

George Maloney

Grant, we beseech you, O Lord our God, that in
whatever dangers we are placed we may call upon
your name, and that when deliverance is given us

from on high we may never cease your praise; through Jesus Christ our Lord.

Leonine Sacramentary

O Lord, our God, grant us, we beseech you, patience in troubles, humility in comforts, constancy in temptations, and victory over all our spiritual foes. Grant us sorrow for our sins, thankfulness for your benefits, fear of your judgment, love of your mercies, and mindfulness of your presence; now and for ever.

John Cosin

Patience in suffering

O my dear Lord, though I am not fit to ask thee for suffering as a gift, and have no strength to do so, at least I will beg of thee grace to meet suffering well, when thou in thy love and wisdom dost bring it upon me.

John Henry Newman

Since thou hast taken from me all that I had of thee, yet of thy grace leave that gift which every dog has by nature: that of being true in my distress, when I am deprived of any consolation.

Saint Mechtilde

Respect and concern for others

Grant me, O Lord, an understanding heart, that I may see into the hearts of your people, and know their strengths and weaknesses, their hopes and their despairs, their efforts and failures, their need of love and their need to love. Through my touch with them grant comfort and hope, and the assurance that new life begins at any age and on any day, redeeming the past, sanctifying the present, and brightening the

future with the assurance of your unfailing love,
brought to me in Jesus Christ, your Son my Lord.

George Appleton

Grant me to recognise in other men, Lord God,
the radiance of your own face.

Teilhard de Chardin

God, help me to be human. Help me to be able to
appreciate and bring out the best in everyone around
me. You have created man, so that he is capable to
appreciate consciously all the gifts that you have given
him. Lord, help me to appreciate all that you have
given me. Help me to be truly human.

Teenagers' Prayer from Harare, Zimbabwe

Lord, teach me to respect people, to accept each
person as unique and created by you. Some people
seem so unattractive that I find it extremely difficult to
see you in them. Yet if I could see myself as others see
me, perhaps I would be less critical and more
understanding. Of your goodness give me compassion
for myself and for others, and never let me give up
trying for the sake of your Son, who genuinely loved
and cared about sinners and outcasts.

Michael Hollings–Etta Gullick

Give us patience and fortitude to put self aside for you
in the most unlikely people: to know that every man's
and any man's suffering is our own first business, for
which we must be willing to go out of our way and to
leave our own interests.

Caryll Houselander

Unselfishness

O Lord, do not let us turn into 'broken cisterns', that can hold no water. Do not let us be so blinded by the enjoyment of the good things of earth that our hearts become insensitive to the cry of the poor, of the sick, of orphaned children and of those innumerable brothers of ours who lack the necessary minimum to eat, to clothe their nakedness, and to gather their family together under one roof.

Pope John XXIII

Help me, O Lord, so to strive and so to act that those things which cloud my own way may not darken the path which others have to tread. Give me unselfish courage so that I am ready always to share my bread and wine, and yet able to hide my hunger and thirst.

Leslie Weatherhead

Lord, to love is to meet oneself, and to meet oneself one must be willing to leave oneself and go towards another. To love is to commune, and to commune one must forget oneself for another. One must die to self completely for another. Loving hurts, for since the fall to love is to crucify self for another. Teach me how to love.

Michel Quoist

Humility

O God, you reject the proud and welcome the humble. Give us true humility, such as your only-begotten Son showed in himself as a pattern for his followers. May we never provoke your wrath by pride, but rather receive your gifts of grace as servants.

True use of freedom

God our Father, whose law is a law of liberty, grant us
wisdom to use aright the freedom which you have
given us, by surrendering ourselves to your service,
knowing that, when we are your willing bondsmen,
then only are we truly free; for Jesus Christ's sake.

Use of talents and possessions

Heavenly Father, your Son Jesus Christ has taught us
that all our possessions and talents are on trust from
you, help us to be zealous and faithful stewards of all
you have given us, so that, true to your grace, we may
merit to be welcomed into your kingdom as good and
faithful servants, who have in all things sought and
accomplished your holy will.

Michael Buckley

Wholehearted repentance

Almighty and most gentle God, when your chosen
people were thirsty you drew a stream of water from a
rock. From our stony hearts draw tears of sorrow,
giving us the grace to weep for our sins and win your
merciful forgiveness.

Forgiveness of sin

We beseech you, Lord, to listen to our humble prayers:
be merciful towards the sinfulness of us who confess
our misdeeds, and in your goodness forgive us and set
our minds at rest.

Community spirit

O God, teach us to live together in love and joy and
peace, to check all bitterness, to disown
discouragement, to practice thanksgiving, and to leap
with joy to any task for others. Strengthen the good

things thus begun, that with gallant and high-hearted happiness we may look for your kingdom in the wills of men.

The Prayer of Toc H

O God, who has bound us together in this bundle of life, give us grace to understand how our lives depend on the courage, the industry, the honesty and the integrity of our fellow men; that we may be mindful of their needs, grateful for their faithfulness and faithful in our responsibilities to them; through Jesus Christ our Lord.

Reinhold Niebuhr

Charity
O God, you make all things work together for the good of those who love you. Kindle the abiding fire of your charity in our hearts, that the longings you inspire in us may not be stifled by any temptation.

Charitable speech
Set a watch, Lord, upon our tongue, that we may never speak the cruel word which is not true; or being true, is not the whole truth; or being wholly true, is merciless; for the love of Jesus Christ our Lord.

Compassion
Give me the grace to be compassionate with sinners from the depths of my heart. May I not be arrogant with him but weep together with him. Grant that, weeping over my neighbour, I may also weep over myself.

Awareness of baptism
Lord God, by our baptism into the body of Christ you have given us a new beginning, a new kind of life. We

know that much of our life, our thoughts, feelings and actions has not yet been touched or changed by the new life you have given: help us to see the claims of your love in every part of our life, and having seen them to accept them, so that everything in us may be remade by your love. Through Jesus Christ our Lord.

Love of the Bible
Lord, who can grasp all the wealth of just one of your words? What we understand in the Bible is much less than what we leave behind, like thirsty people who drink from a fountain. For your word has many shades of meaning, just as those who study it have many different points of view. You have coloured your words with many hues so that each person who studies it can see in it what he loves. You have hidden many treasures in your word so that each of us is enriched as we meditate on it.

Saint Ephraim

Write upon our hearts, O Lord God, the lessons of thy holy Word, and grant that we all may be doers of the same, and not forgetful hearers only.

A. Campbell Fraser

Correct attitude to the world
O Lord, grant that we may not be conformed to the world, but may love it and serve it. Grant that we may never shrink from being instruments of your peace because of the judgment of the world. Grant that we may love you without fear of the world, grant that we may never believe that the inexpressible majesty of yourself may be found in any power of this earth. May we firstly love you and our neighbours as ourselves. May we remember the poor and the prisoner, and the sick and the lonely, and the young searchers, and the

tramps and vagabonds, and the lost and lonely, as we remember Christ, who is in them all.

Alan Paton

The use of time

Lord, time is your gift to me and through it, you who are eternal, enter my life and world. Guide, inspire and help me to fill every moment of every hour, full to the brim with your presence, so that it may overflow to others round me and quench their thirst for a true meaning to life.

Michael Buckley

Lord, help me use time well, especially when I am waiting for my next task just as you waited in Nazareth before beginning your public life, and during that time grew daily in age and wisdom before God and men.

Michael Buckley

Work

Lord, give me the grace to work to bring about the things that I pray for.

Saint Thomas More

Lord give me faith to believe that all work, however humble, is sanctified by your presence when we offer it to the Father, just as you offered your lowly work as a carpenter in Nazareth to the glory of his name.

Michael Buckley

As tools come to be sharpened by the blacksmith, so may we come, O Lord. As sharpened tools go back with their owner, so may we go back to our everyday life and work, to be used by thee, O Lord.

Prayer of Zande Christians

Respect for animals

God, loving creator of all life, help us to treat with
compassion the living creatures entrusted to our care;
may they never be subjected to cruelty and neglect,
and may the dominion you gave us over them be a
partnership of mutual service so that through them we
come to a greater appreciation of your glory in
creation.

Michael Buckley

Prayers in times of sickness and healing

Redemptive use of suffering

O Christ, my Lord, who for my sins did hang upon a
   tree,
grant that your grace in me, poor wretch, may still
   ingrafted be.
Grant that your naked hanging there may kill in me all
   pride,
and care of wealth since you did then in such poor
   state abide.
Grant that your crown of prickling thorns, which you
   for me did wear,
may make me willing for your sake all shame and pain
   to bear.
Grant that your pierced hand, which did of nothing all
   things frame,
may move me to lift up my hands and ever praise your
   name.
Grant that your wounded feet, whose steps were
   perfect evermore,
may learn my feet to tread those paths which you have
   gone before.
Grant that your blessed grave, wherein your body lay
   awhile,
may bury all such vain delights as may my mind defile.

Grant, Lord, that your ascending then may lift my
    mind to thee,
that there my heart and joy may rest, though here in
    flesh I be.

Saint Philip Howard*

O tree of Calvary,
send your roots deep down
into my heart.
Gather together the soil of my heart,
the sands of my fickleness,
the mud of my desires.
Bind them all together,
O tree of Calvary,
interlace them with thy strong roots,
entwine them with the network
of thy love.

A Prayer of an Indian Christian

Facing pain

Father, the world is full of pain; each of us has a share;
for some it is a slight burden, for others it is crushing.
But every Christian can turn it into a blessing if he will
seek the companionship of Christ in his sufferings;
then the pain becomes a new point of fellowship with
Christ; and even our suffering becomes part of the
price of the world's redemption as we fill up what is
left over of the suffering of Christ.

Pain does not then cease to be pain; but it ceases to be
barren pain; and with fellowship with Christ upon the
cross we find new strength for bearing it and even
making it the means by which our hearts are more
fully cleansed of selfishness and grow towards perfect
love. Accomplish this in us through Christ our Lord.

William Temple

Coping with pain

Lord, we do not ask you to rid us of pain but in your mercy grant that our pain may be free from waste, unfretted by rebellion against your will, unsoiled by thought of ourselves, purified by love of others, and ennobled by devotion to your kingdom through the merits of your only Son, our Lord.

Robert Nash

Suffering with Jesus

O crucified Jesus, in giving me your cross give me too your spirit of love and self-abandonment; grant that I may think less of my suffering than of the happiness of suffering with you. What do I suffer that you have not suffered? Or rather what do I suffer at all, if I dare to compare myself with you? O Lord, grant that I may love you and then I shall no longer fear the cross.

François Fénelon

The power of suffering

Lord, make us realise that by simply suffering for Jesus' sake and by bearing 'about our bodies the dying of Jesus' we can often do more for him and for others than we can by being active. It is very hard to understand this, so please make us realise that our very helplessness can be of great use to others, if we suffer it with and for Jesus.

Our suffering works mysteriously, first in ourselves by a kind of renewal and also in others who are perhaps far away, without our ever knowing what we are accomplishing. Christ on the cross has perhaps done more for humanity than Christ speaking and acting in Galilee or Jerusalem. Suffering creates life. It transforms everything it touches. Help us to understand this through Christ, our Lord.

Elizabeth Leseur

Lord Jesus, teach me to realise that all pain is taken up into the saving power of your resurrection and just as you suffered, even death itself, to the Father's glory so may my lesser sufferings be one with yours for the salvation of the world.

Michael Buckley

The help of the Holy Spirit

Grant, Lord, that as you sent this sickness to me, you will also send your Holy Spirit into my heart so that my present illness may be sanctified and used as a school in which I may learn to know the greatness of my misery and the riches of your mercy. May I be so humbled at my misery that I despair not of your mercy and thus renounce all confidence in myself and every other creature so that I may put the whole of my salvation in your all-sufficient merits.

Lewis Bayley

Patience in suffering

Father,
Your Son accepted our sufferings
to teach us the virtue of patience in human illness.
Hear the prayers we offer for our sick brothers and sisters.
May all who suffer pain, illness or disease
realise that they are chosen to be saints,
and know that they are joined in Christ
in his sufferings for the salvation of the world.

Lord, teach me the art of patience while I am well, and give me the use of it when I am sick. In that day either lighten my burden or strengthen my back. Make me, who so often in my health have discovered my weakness, to be strong in my sickness when I solely rely on your assistance.

Thomas Fuller

Inner strength

Let me not pray to be sheltered from dangers but to be fearless in facing them.

Let me not beg for the stilling of my pain but for the heart to conquer it.

Let me not crave in anxious fear to be saved but hope for the patience to win my freedom.

Grant me that I may not be a coward, feeling your mercy in my success alone; but let me find the grasp of your hand in my failure.

Rabindranath Tagore

Resignation in illness

God, you are a loving Father who will not cause us a needless tear; give us then a peaceful heart at rest in the present trouble which afflicts us and which we offer to you in union with the sufferings of Christ, your Son. May we concentrate more on your love and care rather than our own selfish preoccupation with physical pain and emotional disturbance. You know the right time to lift the burden that oppresses us and so we place the present moment, as we do our whole lives, in your tender care. Put your rest in our minds and your peace in our hearts.

Michael Buckley

O good Jesus, I offer and resign myself to you in perfect readiness of will to bear the affliction which I foresee coming upon me. I will accept it with unshaken will as from your hand and I will bear it with all the patience I can, in union with the love with which you bore all your afflictions as coming from your Father's hand and offered them in gratitude to him. I pray that you would grant me fortitude and patience to bear my suffering with gallantry to the

227

praise of your eternal glory and the peace of all the world.

Saint Gertrude

The sick and handicapped
Lord, heal your servants who are sick, and put their trust in you.

Send them help, O Lord, and comfort from your holy place.

Let us pray

Almighty and everlasting God, the eternal salvation of those who believe in you, hear us on behalf of your servants who are sick, for whom we humbly beg the help of your mercy. May their health be restored if you see that it is good for them, and may they give you thanks in your Church.
Through Christ our Lord. **Amen.**

For trust
O loving Father, we pray for all who are handicapped in the race of life; the blind, the defective and the delicate and all who are permanently injured. We pray for those worn out with sickness and those who are wasted with misery, for the dying and all unhappy children. May they learn the mystery of the road of suffering which Christ has trodden and the saints have followed, and bring you this gift that angels cannot bring, a heart that trusts you even in the dark; and this we ask in the name of him who himself took our infirmities upon him, even the same Jesus, our Saviour.

A. S. T. Fisher

For those who nurse the sick

Lord, I thank you that in your love you have taken
from me all earthly riches, and that you now clothe
and feed me through the kindness of others. Lord, I
thank you, that since you have taken from me the sight
of my eyes, you serve me now with the eyes of others.

Lord, I thank you that since you have taken away the
power of my hands and my heart, you serve me by the
hands and hearts of others. Lord, I pray for them.
Reward them for it in your heavenly love, that they
may faithfully serve and please you till they reach a
happy end.

Saint Mechtilde

God's presence in suffering

Father, you do not protect us against catastrophes but
in them you come to our aid. It is in the very midst of
the tempest and misfortune that a wonderful zone of
peace, serenity and joy bursts in us if we dwell in your
grace. You do not help us before we have helped
ourselves, but when we are at the end of our resources
you manifest yourself, and we begin to know that you
have been there all the time.

Louis Evely

Failing health and old age

When the signs of age begin to mark my body and still
more when they touch my mind; when the illness that
is to diminish me or carry me off strikes from without
or is born within me; when the painful moment comes
in which I suddenly awaken to the fact that I am ill or
growing old; in all those dark moments, O God, grant
that I may understand that it is you, provided only my
faith is strong enough, who are painfully parting the
fibres of my being in order to penetrate to the very

marrow of my substance and bear me away within yourself.

Teilhard de Chardin

Healing

O Lord, the healer of our diseases, who knows that the sick have need of a physician; bless all whom you have called to be sharers in your own work of healing with health alike of body and soul, that they may learn their art in dependence upon you, and exercise it always under your sanction, and your honour and glory, who live and reign with the Holy Spirit, ever one God, world without end. Amen.

Sursum Corda

The healing power of the holy name

Jesus, your coming on earth was like a new dawn over a world of darkness: the blind saw, the lame walked again, the sick were healed and even the dead were raised to life. Come again into the lives of everyone and heal the wounds of their broken hearts. Come again to all who are sick or depressed and fill their lives with hope and peace. Come again to us as we call on your holy name so that we too may receive your help and healing grace.

Michael Buckley

God, our Father, you sent your only Son Jesus, on earth to heal a broken-hearted and wounded world. He had compassion on those who called on him for help and healing. He touched the sick and guilt-laden, and they walked away in health and freedom of Spirit. Visit us now with his saving power so that we too may be released in mind and body to praise your healing grace through Christ our Lord.

Michael Buckley

God, we witness unheard of things. You, God, have given power to Jesus of Nazareth, whom we recognise as one of us, to be merciful to others and to forgive them. We ask you, God, for this power, this freedom to be a healing grace to all who live in this world, as a sign that you are the forgiveness of sins.

A Christian's Prayer Book

God, our Father, your Son gave more than he was asked for to those who pleaded with him for healing. People asked for health of body and he released them from their sins as well; he touched their skin and healed the deep wounds of the spirit. May we be touched by the same healing power and thus be released from the hidden forces deep within us which hold us back from true health of mind and body.

Michael Buckley

Lord Jesus, you are the great friend of the sick,
and you healed them while you were on earth.
Grant them once more your healing power and
    comfort them in their affliction.
Come, Holy Spirit, strengthen them so that they may
    find renewed health
    both in soul and body.

Lord Jesus Christ, who slept on a storm-tossed lake, grant me the gift of sleep so that with a mind at peace, a heart at rest, and a body relaxed I may use my sleeping hours for healing and waken strengthened to renew my tasks with brighter vision, confidence and hope.

Michael Buckley

A blessing for the sick

Lord Jesus, when you were on earth, they brought the sick to you and you healed them all. Today we ask you to bless all those in sickness, in weakness and in pain;

Those who are blind and who cannot see the light of the sun; the beauty of the world, or the faces of their friends;

those who are deaf and cannot hear the voices which speak to them;

those who are helpless and who must lie in bed while others go out and in.

Bless all such.

Those whose minds have lost their reason;

those who are so nervous that they cannot cope with life;

those who worry about everything.

Bless all such.

Those who must face life under some handicap;

those whose weakness means that they must always be careful;

those who are lame and maimed and cannot enter into any of the strenuous activities or pleasures of life.

Bless all such.

Grant that we in our health and our strength may never find those who are weak and handicapped a nuisance, but grant that we may always do and give all that we can to help them, and to make life easier for them.

William Barclay

Act of resignation of death

O Lord, my God, I now at this moment, readily and willingly accept at your hand whatever kind of death it may please you to send me, with all its pains, and sorrows. Through Christ, Our Lord. Amen.

Lord Jesus, today we accept from your merciful hands what is to come. The times of trial in this world, the suffering of our death, the sorrow and loneliness of our last hours upon earth, the purifying, unknown pains of our purgatory. Into your hands, O Lord, into your hands, we commit our living and dying, knowing that you are the dawn of eternal day, the burning light of the morning star.

Caryll Houselander

For the dying
O most merciful Jesus, lover of souls: I pray you by the agony of your most Sacred Heart, and by the sorrows of your Immaculate Mother, cleanse in your own blood the sinners of the whole world who are now in their agony, and are to die this day. May they be comforted by the hope of the resurrection.

Heart of Jesus, once in agony, pity the dying.

Jesus, I ask you to pour down your blessing on the dying. Give them grace to bear their sickness, and strength to conform themselves to your blessed will. Pity them and help them by your mercy, that in the final hour they may not lose courage, but may have fortitude to fight the good fight for you to the end.

God of power and mercy,
you have made death itself
the gateway to eternal life.
Look with love on our dying brother (sister),
and make him (her) one with your Son in his
    sufferings and death,
that sealed with the blood of Christ,
he (she) may come before you free from sin.

Final perseverance

Grant, we beseech you, O Lord, that in the hour of our death we may be refreshed by your holy sacraments and delivered from all guilt, and so deserve to be received with joy into the arms of your mercy.

Mother of sorrows, by the anguish and love with which you stood beneath the cross of Jesus, stand by me in my last moments. To your maternal heart I commend the last hours of my life; offer these hours to the eternal Father in union with the passion of our dearest Lord. Offer frequently, in atonement for my sins, and in gratitude for the resurrection, the precious blood of Jesus, shed on Calvary, to obtain for me the grace to receive holy communion before my death, and to breathe forth my soul in the actual presence of Jesus in the blessed sacrament; and when the moment of my death has at length arrived, and I stand on the threshold of heaven, present me as your child to Jesus; say to him on my behalf 'Father, receive him/her this day into your kingdom'.

Jesus, I live for you;
Jesus, I die for you;
Jesus, I am yours in life and in death.

At judgment time

Have pity upon every man, Lord, in that hour when he has finished his task and stands before thee like a child, whose hands are being examined.

Paul Claudel

Mary, Mother of the Church

Mary has always had a special place in Christian devotion, perhaps nowhere more pronounced than in the Eastern Church. The reason all generations shall call her blessed *is because God chose her to be the mother of his Son. By her obedience to his will she set in physical motion the work of our redemption. The Word was made flesh in her, and mankind was once more restored to God's favour. Mother of the physical body of Jesus Christ, she is also the spiritual mother of the Church, a title given to her by the bishops of the Second Vatican Council. We honour her and ask her intercession because of her unique relationship with God the Father and Holy Spirit through her Son.*

Prayers to Our Lady

Hail holy Queen
Hail, holy Queen, mother of Mercy.
Hail, our life, our sweetness and our hope.
To thee do we cry, poor banished children of Eve;
to thee do we send up our sighs, mourning and
weeping,
in this vale of tears.
Turn then, most gracious advocate, thine eyes of mercy
towards us;
and after this our exile, show unto us the blessed
fruit of thy womb, Jesus. O clement, O loving,
O sweet virgin Mary.

Pray for us, O holy mother of God.

**That we may be made worthy of the promises of
Christ.**

Let us pray:
Almighty, everlasting God, who, through the working
of the Holy Spirit, prepared the body and soul of the
glorious virgin Mary to be a worthy dwelling for thy
Son: grant that we who remember her with joy may be
delivered by her prayers from the evils that beset us in
this world and from everlasting death in the next.
Through the same Christ our Lord. **Amen.**

The Memorare
Remember, O most loving virgin Mary, that never was
it known that anyone who fled to your protection,
implored your help, or sought your intercession was
left unaided. Inspired by this confidence, we fly unto
you, O virgin of virgins, our mother. To you we come,
before you we stand, sinful and sorrowful. O mother
of the Word incarnate, despise not our petitions, but in
your mercy hear and answer me.

Saint Bernard

The Angelus
The angel of the Lord declared unto Mary:
And she conceived of the Holy Spirit.
Hail Mary . . .
Behold the handmaid of the Lord:
Be it done unto me according to your word.
Hail Mary . . .
And the Word was made flesh:
And dwelt among us.
Hail Mary . . .
Pray for us, O holy mother of God
That we may be worthy of the promises of Christ.

Let us pray
Pour forth, we beseech you, O Lord, your grace into
our hearts, that we, to whom the incarnation of Christ,

your Son, was made known by the message of an angel, may be brought by his passion and cross to the glory of his resurrection, through the same Christ our Lord. **Amen.**

May the divine assistance remain always with us and may the souls of the faithful departed, through the mercy of God, rest in peace. **Amen.**

The Regina Caeli (said in Paschal time)
O Queen of heaven, rejoice! Alleluia.
For he whom you did merit to bear, Alleluia.
Has risen as he said. Alleluia.
Pray for us to God. Alleluia.

Rejoice and be glad, O virgin Mary, Alleluia.
For the Lord has risen indeed. Alleluia.

Let us pray
O God, who gave joy to the world through the resurrection of your Son our Lord Jesus Christ, grant that we may obtain, through his virgin mother, Mary, the joys of everlasting life. Through the same Christ our Lord. **Amen.**

For the conversion of our nation
O blessed virgin Mary, mother of God, and our most gentle queen and mother, look down in mercy upon our nation, and upon us all who greatly hope and trust in you.

By you it was that Jesus, our Saviour and our hope, was given to the world, he has given you to us that we might hope still more. Plead for us your children, whom you did receive and accept at the foot of the cross, O sorrowful mother.

Intercede for our separated brothers and sisters, that with us in the one true fold, they may be united to the chief shepherd, the vicar of your Son. Pray for us all, dear mother, that by faith fruitful in good works, we may all deserve to see and praise God, together with you, in our heavenly home. Amen.

Our Lady of Perpetual Succour
Most holy virgin Mary, who, to inspire me with boundless confidence, has been pleased to take that name, Mother of Perpetual Succour, I beseech you to aid me at all times and in all places; in my temptations, in my difficulties, in all the miseries of life, and, above all, at the hour of my death so that I may share in the resurrection of your Son our Lord Jesus Christ. Grant most charitable mother, that I may remember you at all times, and always have recourse to you; for I am sure that, if I am faithful in invoking you, you will promptly come to my aid. Obtain for me, therefore, the grace to pray to you unceasingly with filial confidence, and that, by virtue of this constant prayer, I may obtain your perpetual help and persevere in the practice of my faith. Bless me most tender mother, ever ready to aid me, and pray for me now and at the hour of my death.
Mother of Perpetual Succour, protect also all those whom I recommend to you, the Church, the Holy Father, our country, my family, my friends and enemies, especially all those who suffer.

Our Lady of Good Counsel
Most glorious virgin, chosen by the eternal counsel to be the mother of the eternal Word made flesh, treasure of divine grace and advocate of sinners, I, the most unworthy of your servants, beseech you to be my guide and counsellor in this vale of tears. Obtain for

me by the most precious blood of your Son, the pardon of my sins, the salvation of my soul, and the means necessary to obtain it. Grant that the holy Catholic Church may triumph over the enemies of the gospel, and that the kingdom of Christ may be propagated on earth.

Our Lady of Lourdes

Ever immaculate Virgin, Mother of mercy, health of the sick, refuge of sinners, comfort of the afflicted, you know my needs, my troubles, my sufferings; cast on me a look of pity. By appearing in the grotto of Lourdes, you were pleased to make it a privileged sanctuary, from which you dispense your favours, and already many sufferers have obtained the cure of their infirmities, both spiritual and physical. I come, therefore, with the most unbounded confidence to implore your maternal intercession. Obtain most loving mother, my requests, through Jesus Christ your Son our Lord. Amen.

The prayers of Fatima

These prayers are to be recited after each decade of the rosary.

O my Jesus, forgive us our sins, save us from the fires of hell. Lead all souls to heaven, especially those in greatest need.

O Jesus, it is for your love, for the conversion of sinners, and in reparation for the sins committed against the immaculate heart of Mary (when offering a penance).

My God, I believe, I adore, I hope and I love you. I ask pardon for those who do not believe, do not adore, do not hope, and do not love you.

Conversion of Sinners

Most Holy Trinity, Father, Son and Holy Spirit, I adore you, profoundly, and I offer you the most precious body, blood, soul and divinity of Jesus Christ present in all the tabernacles of the world in reparation for the outrages, sacrileges and indifferences with which he is offended, and by the infinite merits of his most Sacred Heart and of the immaculate heart of Mary I ask you for the conversion of all sinners.

The Ave Maria of Saint Mechtilde

Hail, thou unique offspring of the omnipotence of the Father, of the wisdom of the Son, and of the goodness of the Holy Spirit, *Mary*, who dost fill heaven and earth with thy gentle light. Thou that art *full of grace, the Lord is with thee*, even the only-begotten Son of the Father, and the one only Son of the love of thy virgin heart, thy sweetest spouse and thy beloved. *Blessed art thou among women* for thou hast banished the curse of Eve and hast brought back an everlasting blessing. *And blessed is the fruit of thy womb, Jesus*, the Lord and creator of all things, who doth evermore bless and sanctify, enrich and give life to all things.

Holy Mary, succour the wretched, help the disheartened, put new heart into the feeble. Pray for the people, intervene for the clergy, intercede for all holy women. May all those who honour your memory, experience your generous help. Promptly you attend to the voice of those who pray to you and satisfy the desire of each one. Let your undertaking be diligent intercession for the people of God, for you have merited, to bear the ransom of the world, he who lives and reigns for ever.

Fulbert of Chartres

O Mary, help me to live as a faithful disciple of Jesus, for the building up of Christian society and the joy of the Catholic Church. I greet you, mother, morning and evening; I pray to you as I go upon my way; from you I hope for the inspiration and encouragement that will enable me to fulfil the sacred promises of my earthly vocation, give glory to God and win eternal salvation, O Mary! Like you in Bethlehem and on Golgotha, I too wish to stay always close to Jesus. He is the eternal King of all ages and all peoples.

Pope John XXIII

O, that the soul of Mary were in us to glorify the Lord! That the spirit of Mary were in us to rejoice in God.

Saint Ambrose

Thirty days prayer to the Blessed Virgin Mary in honour of the sacred passion of our Lord Jesus Christ

It has long been a custom in the Church to say this prayer of petition on thirty consecutive days. It is also recommended as a Lenten devotion as well as for all Fridays throughout the year, because it concentrates on our Lord's saving passion.

Ever-glorious and blessed Mary, queen of virgins, Mother of mercy, through that sword of sorrow which pierced your tender heart whilst your only Son, Jesus Christ, our Lord, suffered death and ignominy on the cross; through that filial tenderness and pure love he has for you, while from his cross he recommended you to the care and protection of his beloved disciple, Saint John, take pity, I beseech you, on my poverty and need; have compassion on my anxieties and cares;

assist and comfort me in all my infirmities and miseries. You are the mother of mercies, the only refuge of the needy and the orphan, of the desolate and afflicted.

Cast therefore an eye of pity on this sorrowful child of Eve, and hear my prayer; for since, in just punishment of my sins, I find myself surrounded by a multitude of evils, and oppressed with much anguish of spirit, where can I fly for more secure shelter, O loving mother of my Lord and Saviour Jesus Christ, than under the wings of your maternal protection? Listen, therefore, I beseech you, with an air of pity and compassion, to my humble and earnest request.

I ask it, through the infinite mercy of your dear Son: through that love and humility with which he embraced our human nature, when through your own obedience to the divine will, you consented to become his mother and whom after nine months, you brought forth from your chaste womb, to visit this world, and bless it with his presence. I ask it, through the anguish of mind of your beloved Son, our dear Saviour, on Mount Olivet, when he besought his eternal Father, to remove from him, if possible, the bitter chalice of his future passion. I ask it, through the threefold repetition of his prayers in the garden, from whence afterwards in sorrow you accompanied him to the scene of his death and sufferings.

I ask it, through the laceration of his sinless flesh, caused by the cords and whips with which he was bound and scourged, when stripped of his seamless garments, for which his executioners afterwards cast lots. I ask it, through the scoffs and ignominies by which he was insulted; the false accusations and unjust sentence by which he was condemned to death, and which he bore with enduring patience. I ask it,

through his bitter tears and bloody sweat; his silence and resignation; his sadness and grief of heart.

I ask it, through the blood which trickled from his royal and sacred head, when struck with the sceptre of a reed, and pierced with his crown of thorns. I ask it, through the excruciating torments he suffered, when his hands and feet were fastened with nails to the tree of the cross. I ask it, through his unbearable thirst, and bitter potion of vinegar and gall. I ask it, through his dereliction on the cross, when he exclaimed: *My God, my God, why have you forsaken me?* I ask it, through his mercy extended to the good thief, and through his recommending his precious soul and spirit into the hands of his eternal Father, before he expired, saying: *All is consummated.* I ask it, through the blood mixed with water, which issued from his sacred side when pierced with a lance from whence a flood of grace and mercy has flowed to us.

I ask it, through his immaculate life, bitter passion, and ignominious death on the cross, at which even nature itself was thrown into convulsions by the bursting of rocks, rending of the veil of the temple, the earthquake, and darkness, of the sun and moon. I ask it, through his glorious victory over death, when he arose again to life on the third day, and through the joy which his appearance for forty days gave you, his blessed mother, his apostles, and the rest of his disciples; when in your and their presence, he miraculously ascended into heaven.

I ask it, through the grace of the Holy Spirit, infused into the hearts of his disciples; when he descended upon them in the form of fiery tongues, and by which they were inspired with zeal for the conversion of the world, when they went to preach the gospel. I ask it, through the glorious appearance of your Son, at the last day, when he shall come to judge the living and the dead, and the world by fire. I ask it, through the compassion he bore you in this life, and the wonderful joy you felt at your assumption into heaven where you eternally contemplate his divine perfection.

O glorious and ever blessed virgin, comfort the heart of your suppliant, by obtaining for me

here mention or reflect on your request.

And as I believe that my divine Saviour honours you as his beloved mother, to whom he refuses nothing, because you ask nothing contrary to his honour, so let me soon experience your powerful intercession. Wherefore, O most blessed virgin, beside my present petition, and whatever else I may stand in need of, obtain for me also of your dear Son, our Lord and our God, a lively faith, firm hope, perfect charity, true contrition of heart and genuine tears of compunction, sincere confession, satisfaction and deliverance from sin, love of God and my neighbour, a correct attitude to the world, patience to suffer insults, even death itself, for love of your Son, our Saviour Jesus Christ. Obtain likewise for me, O holy mother of God, perseverance in good works, the carrying-out of my good resolutions, mortification of my self-will, a holy life, and, at my last moments, a strong and sincere repentance, with such presence of mind, as will enable me to receive the last sacrament of the Church worthily, so as to die in God's friendship and favour.

Lastly, I beseech you, for the souls of my parents, brethren, relatives and benefactors, both living and dead, life everlasting, from the only giver of every good and perfect gift, the Lord God almighty: to whom be all power, now and for ever. Amen.

The Rosary

An integral part of Catholic devotional practice since before the thirteenth century, the rosary recalls the principal mysteries of our salvation in groups of five decades (chaplets). Each group of five decades is preceded by the recitation of the Creed, and three Hail Marys for an increase in faith, hope and charity. It concludes with a recitation of one of the anthems to Our Lady appropriate to the liturgical season. The repetition of the prayers of each decade, one Our Father, ten Hail Marys and one Glory be to the Father, helps us to meditate deeply on God's love for us.

Come, Holy Spirit, fill the hearts of the faithful
and kindle in them the fire of your love.

Send forth your Spirit.
And you will renew the face of the earth.

Let us pray
O God, who taught the hearts of the faithful by the light of the Holy Spirit, grant that, by the gift of the same Spirit, we may be always truly wise and ever rejoice in his consolation. Through Christ our Lord.
Amen.

THE JOYFUL MYSTERIES

Usually said on Mondays and Thursdays throughout the year and on Sundays from Advent to the beginning of Lent.

1 The Annunciation
Let us contemplate in this mystery how the angel Gabriel saluted our Blessed Lady with the title 'Full of grace', and made known to her that she had been

chosen to be mother of Our Lord and Saviour, Jesus Christ.

Our Father (once), Hail Mary (ten times). Glory be to the Father (once) for each mystery.

2 The Visitation
Let us contemplate in this mystery how the Blessed Virgin Mary, having learned from the angel that her cousin, Elizabeth, had conceived, went with haste into the hill-country to visit her, and remained with her about three months.

3 The Nativity
Let us contemplate in this mystery how the Blessed Virgin Mary, with joy, brought forth our Lord, Jesus Christ, *wrapped him in swaddling clothes, and laid him in a manger, because there was no room for them in the inn* at Bethlehem.

4 The Presentation
Let us contemplate in this mystery how on the day of her purification, the Blessed Virgin Mary, with Joseph, presented the child Jesus in the temple, where holy Simeon with joy received him into his arms, and, with the prophetess Anna, proclaimed him Saviour of the world.

5 The Finding of Jesus in the Temple
Let us contemplate in this mystery how the Blessed Virgin Mary and Joseph, having lost the child Jesus in Jerusalem, sought him for three days, and at length, to their great joy found him in the temple *sitting in the midst of the doctors, hearing them and asking them questions.*

Usually said on Tuesdays and Fridays throughout the year and on Sundays in Lent.

1 The agony in the Garden
Let us contemplate in this mystery how our Lord, Jesus Christ, was so afflicted for us in the garden of Gethsemane that *his sweat became as drops of blood trickling down upon the ground.*

2 The scourging of Jesus
Let us contemplate in this mystery how our Lord, Jesus Christ, was, by Pilate's most unjust and cruel sentence, bound to a pillar and scourged.

3 The crowning with thorns
Let us contemplate in this mystery how Pilate's soldiers clothed our Lord, Jesus Christ, with purple, *and plaiting a crown of thorns they put it on his head and bowing the knee before him, they mocked him.*

4 The carrying of the Cross
Let us contemplate in this mystery how our Lord, Jesus Christ, having been sentenced to die, patiently bore the cross which was laid upon him for his greater torment and ignominy.

5 The Crucifixion
Let us contemplate in this mystery how our Lord, Jesus Christ, being come to 'the place of Calvary', was stripped of his clothes, on which after three hours of agony, he expired in the presence of his most afflicted mother.

Usually said on Wednesdays, Saturdays and also on Sundays from Easter to Advent.

1 **The Resurrection**
Let us contemplate in this mystery how our Lord, Jesus Christ, triumphing gloriously over death, rose again, the third day, immortal never to suffer again.

2 **The Ascension**
Let us contemplate in this mystery how our Lord, Jesus Christ, forty days after his resurrection, ascended into heaven, in the sight of his holy mother, and of his Apostles and disciples.

3 **The descent of the Holy Spirit**
Let us contemplate in this mystery how our Lord, Jesus Christ, being seated on the right hand of the Father, sent, as he had promised, the Holy Ghost upon his apostles, who on their return to Jerusalem, after the ascension, had persevered in prayer, with the Blessed Virgin Mary, awaiting the fulfilment of his promise.

4 **The Assumption**
Let us contemplate in this mystery how the Blessed Virgin Mary, having passed out of this world, was assumed both body and soul into heaven by her divine Son.

5 **The Coronation of Our Lady**
Let us contemplate in this mystery how the Blessed Virgin Mary, amid the great jubilee and exultation of the whole court of heaven, was crowned by her divine Son with the brightest diadem of glory.

(If the Litany of Loreto is not said the rosary is concluded as follows:)

Hail Holy Queen

Hail, holy queen, Mother of mercy; hail, our life, our sweetness, and our hope; to thee do we cry, poor banished children of Eve; to thee do we send up our sighs, mourning and weeping in this valley of tears. Turn then, most gracious advocate, thine eyes of mercy towards us; and after this our exile, show unto us the blessed fruit of thy womb, Jesus, O clement, O loving, O sweet Virgin Mary.

Queen of the most holy rosary, pray for us.
That we may be made worthy of the promises of Christ.

Let us pray
O God, whose only-begotten Son, by his life, death and resurrection has purchased for us the rewards of eternal life; grant, we beseech you, that meditating upon these mysteries in the most holy rosary of the Blessed Virgin Mary, we may both imitate what they contain and obtain what they promise, through the same Christ our Lord. Amen.

The Litany of Our Lady (Litany of Loreto)

Lord, have mercy.	**Lord, have mercy.**
Christ, have mercy.	**Christ, have mercy.**
Lord, have mercy.	**Lord, have mercy.**
Christ, hear us.	**Christ, graciously hear us.**
God the Father of heaven,	**have mercy on us.**
God the Son, redeemer of the world,	**have mercy on us.**
God the Holy Spirit,	**have mercy on us.**
Holy Trinity, one God,	**have mercy on us.**

Holy Mary,	**pray for us.**
Holy Mother of God,	**pray for us.**
Holy Virgin of virgins,	**pray for us.**
Mother of Christ,	**pray for us.**
Mother of divine grace,	**pray for us.**
Mother most pure,	**pray for us.**
Mother most chaste,	**pray for us.**
Mother inviolate,	**pray for us.**
Mother undefiled,	**pray for us.**
Mother most lovable,	**pray for us.**
Mother most admirable,	**pray for us.**
Mother of good counsel,	**pray for us.**
Mother of our creator,	**pray for us.**
Mother of our Saviour,	**pray for us.**
Virgin most prudent,	**pray for us.**
Virgin most venerable,	**pray for us.**
Virgin most renowned,	**pray for us.**
Virgin most powerful,	**pray for us.**
Virgin most merciful.	**pray for us.**
Virgin most faithful,	**pray for us.**
Mirror of justice,	**pray for us.**
Seat of wisdom,	**pray for us.**
Cause of our joy,	**pray for us.**
Spiritual vessel,	**pray for us.**
Vessel of honour,	**pray for us.**
Singular vessel of devotion,	**pray for us.**
Mystical rose,	**pray for us.**
Tower of David,	**pray for us.**
Tower of ivory,	**pray for us.**
House of gold,	**pray for us.**
Arc of the covenant,	**pray for us.**
Gate of heaven,	**pray for us.**
Morning star,	**pray for us.**
Health of the sick,	**pray for us.**
Refuge of sinners,	**pray for us.**
Comfort of the afflicted,	**pray for us.**

Help of Christians,	**pray for us.**
Queen of angels,	**pray for us.**
Queen of patriarchs,	**pray for us.**
Queen of prophets,	**pray for us.**
Queen of apostles,	**pray for us.**
Queen of martyrs,	**pray for us.**
Queen of confessors,	**pray for us.**
Queen of virgins,	**pray for us.**
Queen of all saints,	**pray for us.**
Queen conceived without original sin,	**pray for us.**
Queen assumed into heaven,	**pray for us.**
Queen of the most holy rosary,	**pray for us.**
Queen of peace,	**pray for us.**
Lamb of God, you take away the sins of the world,	**spare us, O Lord.**
Lamb of God, you take away the sins of the world,	**graciously hear us, O Lord.**
Lamb of God, you take away the sins of the world,	**have mercy on us.**

Pray for us, O holy Mother of God.
That we may be worthy of the promises of Christ.

Let us pray
Grant that we your servants, Lord, may enjoy unfailing health of mind and body, and through the prayers of the ever Blessed Virgin Mary in her glory, free us from our sorrows in this world and give us eternal happiness in the next. Through Christ our Lord. **Amen.**

The Angels and Saints

The Church militant on earth is linked through Christ's resurrection with the Church triumphant in heaven. We ask their help in our earthly pilgrimage so that we too, one day, may share their glory and destiny. We pray especially for the intercession of the saints and angels whose patron name was given to us in baptism.

Prayers to the Saints

Thanksgiving for the Saints
We thank you, God, for the saints of all ages, for those who in times of darkness kept the lamp of faith burning, for the great souls who saw visions of larger truths and dared to declare them, for the multitude of quiet, gracious souls whose presence purified and sanctified the world; and for those known and loved by us, who have passed from this earthly fellowship into the fuller life with you. Accept this, our thanksgiving, through Jesus Christ, to whom be praise and dominion for ever. Amen.

Fellowship Litanies

For a share with the Saints
O God our Father,
source of all holiness,
the work of your hands is manifest in your saints,
the beauty of your truth is reflected in their faith.

May we, who aspire to have part in their joy,
be filled with the Spirit that blessed their lives,

so that, having shared their faith on earth,
we may also know their peace in your kingdom.

Saint Joseph
To you, O blessed Joseph; we fly in our tribulation and
after imploring the help of your most holy spouse, we
ask also with confidence for your patronage. By the
affection which united you to the Immaculate Virgin,
Mother of God, and the paternal love with which you
embraced the child Jesus, we beseech you to look
kindly upon the inheritance which Jesus Christ
acquired by his precious blood, and by your powerful
aid to help us in our needs.

Protect, most careful guardian of the holy family, the
chosen people of Jesus Christ. Keep us, most loving
father, from all pestilence of error and corruption. Be
mindful of us, most powerful protector, from your
place in heaven, in this warfare with the powers of
darkness; and, as you did snatch the child Jesus from
danger of death, so now defend the holy Church of
God from the snares of the enemy and from all
adversity. Guard each one of us by your perpetual
patronage, so that sustained by your example and
help, we may live in holiness, die a holy death, and
obtain the ever-lasting happiness of heaven. Amen.

God, who was pleased to elect blessed Joseph as
spouse of your Mother; grant we beseech you, that as
we venerate him as our protector on earth we may
deserve to have him as our intercessor in heaven, who
lives and reigns, world without end. Amen.

O glorious Saint Joseph remind all who work that they
are not alone in their labour, their joy or their
sufferings, because Jesus is by their side, with Mary,

his mother and ours, supporting them, wiping the sweat from their brows, and setting a value on their toil. Teach them to use their labour, as you did, as a supreme means of attaining holiness.

Pope John XXIII

Novena for the feast of Saint Joseph the workman (commencing 22nd April)
Glorious Saint Joseph, model of all who are devoted to labour, obtain for me the grace to work conscientiously, putting the call of duty above my selfish interests, to work with gratitude and joy, considering it an honour to employ and develop, by means of labour, the gifts received from God; to work with order, peace, moderation and patience without ever recoiling before weariness or difficulties; to work, above all, with purity of intention, and with detachment from self, as Jesus worked at Nazareth under the direction of your guidance and skill. Amen.

Saint Peter
All-powerful Father,
you have built your Church
on the rock of Saint Peter's confession of faith.
May nothing divide or weaken
our unity in faith and love.

Saint Paul
Glorious Saint Paul, who from a persecutor of the Christian name became an apostle of burning zeal, and who, in order that Jesus Christ might be known to the furthermost bounds of the earth, suffered imprisonment, scourging, stoning, shipwreck, and every kind of persecution, and who finally shed your blood to the last drop. Obtain for us the grace of accepting, as divine favours, the infirmities, torments,

and calamities of this life, so that we may not be drawn from the service of God by the trials of this our exile, but on the contrary may prove ourselves more and more faithful and fervent. **Amen.**

Pray for us, Saint Paul the apostle.
That we may be made worthy of the promises of Christ.

Let us pray.
God, who taught the whole world by the preaching of blessed Paul, the apostle, grant, we beseech you, that we, who celebrate his conversion, may feel the might of his intercession before you. Through Christ our Lord. **Amen.**

Saint Mary Magdalene
Father,
your Son first entrusted to Mary Magdalene
the joyful news of his resurrection;
by her prayers and example
may we proclaim Christ as our living Lord
and one day see him in glory.

Saint Ignatius Loyola
Father,
you gave Saint Ignatius of Loyola to your Church
to bring greater glory to your name.
May we follow his example on earth
and share the crown of life in heaven

Saint John Vianney
Father of mercy,
you made Saint John Vianney outstanding
in his priestly zeal and concern for your people;
by his example and prayers,

enable us to win our brothers and sisters
to the love of Christ
and come with them to eternal glory.

Saint Teresa of Avila
Father,
by your spirit you raised up Saint Teresa of Avila
to show your Church the way to perfection.
May her inspired teaching
awaken in us a longing for true holiness.

Saint Francis Xavier
God our Father,
by the preaching of Francis Xavier
you brought many nations to yourself.
Give his zeal for the faith to all who believe in you,
that your Church may rejoice in continued growth
throughout the world.

Saint John of the Cross
Father,
you endowed John of the Cross with a spirit of
self-denial
and a love of the cross.
By following his example,
may we come to the eternal vision of your glory.

Saint Michael the archangel
Holy Michael, the archangel defend us in the day of
battle; be our safeguard against the wickedness and
snares of the devil. May God rebuke him we humbly
pray; and may the prince of the heavenly host, by the
power of God thrust down to hell Satan and all wicked
spirits, who wander through the world for the ruin of
souls. Amen.

Saint Vincent de Paul,
God our Father,
you gave Vincent de Paul
the courage and holiness of an apostle
for the well-being of the poor
and the formation of the clergy.
Help us to be zealous in continuing his work.

Saint Therese of Liseux
God our Father
you have promised your kingdom
to those who are willing to become like little children.
Help us to follow the way of 'the Little Flower' with
confidence
so that by her prayers
we may come to know your eternal glory.

Saint Francis of Assisi
Father,
You helped Saint Francis to reflect the image of Christ
through a life of poverty and humility.
May we follow your Son
by walking in the footsteps of Francis of Assisi,
and by imitating his joyful love.

Saint Augustine of Hippo
Glorious Saint Augustine, look upon me with
compassion, and pray for me to be a worthy child of
God our loving Father. Let me say with you: *too late
have I known you, too late have I loved you*, so that I may
repair my past sinful life by the most ardent, generous
love for my divine spouse. Ask for me a share in your
profound humility, that I may ever be little and
humble in my eyes, preferring to be made little
account of, in order to resemble him, who underwent
such deep humiliations for the love of me. Obtain also

for me, unbounded courage and confidence, patience and kindness. At the hour of death may I go home to my heavenly Father in your dear company and there may we praise almighty God for all eternity. Amen.

Saint Anthony of Padua

Holy Saint Anthony, gentlest of saints, your love for God and charity for his creatures made you worthy to possess miraculous powers. Miracles waited on your word, which you were ever ready to speak for those in trouble or anxiety. Encouraged by this thought, I implore of you to obtain for me . . . The answer to my prayer may require a miracle, even so, you are the saint of miracles. O gentle and loving Saint Anthony, whose heart was ever full of human sympathy, whisper my petition into the ears of the sweet infant Jesus, who loved to be folded in your arms.

Saint Jude

Saint Jude, glorious apostle, faithful servant and friend of Jesus, the name of the man who betrayed our Saviour has caused you to be forgotten by many. The Church, however, invokes you as the patron of things despaired of; pray for me that I may receive the consolations and the help of heaven in all my necessities, tribulations and sufferings, particularly . . . and that I may bless God with the elect throughout eternity. Amen.

Saint Martin de Porres

Most humble Saint Martin your wonderful love for all who turned to you in need inspires me now to ask your help. I implore you to help me in my present difficulties. I particularly ask you to obtain for me from God . . . May I, by imitating your love and humility, find true peace in my life and perfect resignation to the will of God.

Saint Oliver Plunkett

Glorious martyr who willingly gave your life for your faith, help us also to be strong in faith. May we be always loyal and true to Christ and his vicar on earth. By your intercession and example may all hatred and bitterness be banished from the hearts of all men and women. May the peace of Christ reign in our hearts as it did in your heart, this we ask with complete confidence.

The Litany of the Saints

Lord, have mercy on us.	**Lord, have mercy on us.**
Christ, have mercy on us.	**Christ, have mercy on us.**
Christ, hear us.	**Christ, graciously hear us.**
God, the Father of heaven,	**have mercy on us.**
God, the Son, redeemer of the world,	**have mercy on us.**
God, the Holy Spirit,	**have mercy on us.**
Holy Trinity, one God,	**have mercy on us.**
Holy Mary,	**pray for us.**
Holy Mother of God,	**pray for us.**
Holy Virgin of virgins,	**pray for us.**
Saint Michael,	**pray for us.**
Saint Gabriel,	**pray for us.**
Saint Raphael,	**pray for us.**
All holy angels and archangels,	**pray for us.**
All holy orders of blessed spirits,	**pray for us.**
Saint John the Baptist,	**pray for us.**
Saint Joseph,	**pray for us.**
All holy patriarchs and prophets,	**pray for us.**

Saint Peter,	**pray for us.**
Saint Paul,	**pray for us.**
Saint Andrew,	**pray for us.**
Saint James,	**pray for us.**
Saint John,	**pray for us.**
Saint Thomas,	**pray for us.**
Saint James,	**pray for us.**
Saint Philip,	**pray for us.**
Saint Bartholomew,	**pray for us.**
Saint Matthew,	**pray for us.**
Saint Simon,	**pray for us.**
Saint Thaddeus,	**pray for us.**
Saint Matthias,	**pray for us.**
Saint Barnabas,	**pray for us.**
Saint Luke,	**pray for us.**
Saint Mark,	**pray for us.**
All holy apostles and evangelists,	**pray for us.**
All holy disciples of our Lord,	**pray for us.**
All holy innocents,	**pray for us.**
Saint Stephen,	**pray for us.**
Saint Lawrence,	**pray for us.**
Saint Vincent,	**pray for us.**
Saints Fabian and Sebastian,	**pray for us.**
Saints John and Paul,	**pray for us.**
Saints Cosmas and Damian,	**pray for us.**
Saints Gervase and Protase,	**pray for us.**
All holy martyrs,	**pray for us.**
Saint Sylvester,	**pray for us.**
Saint Gregory,	**pray for us.**
Saint Ambrose,	**pray for us.**
Saint Augustine,	**pray for us.**
Saint Jerome,	**pray for us.**
Saint Martin,	**pray for us.**
Saint Nicholas,	**pray for us.**
All holy bishops and confessors,	**pray for us.**
All holy doctors,	**pray for us.**

Saint Anthony,	**pray for us.**
Saint Benedict,	**pray for us.**
Saint Dominic,	**pray for us.**
Saint Francis,	**pray for us.**
All holy priests and levites,	**pray for us.**
All holy monks and hermits,	**pray for us.**
Saint Mary Magdalen,	**pray for us.**
Saint Agatha,	**pray for us.**
Saint Lucy,	**pray for us.**
Saint Agnes,	**pray for us.**
Saint Cecilia,	**pray for us.**
Saint Catherine,	**pray for us.**
Saint Anastasia,	**pray for us.**
All holy virgins and widows,	**pray for us.**
All holy saints of God,	**make intercession for us.**
Be merciful,	**spare us, O Lord.**
Be merciful,	**graciously hear us, O Lord.**
From all evil,	**deliver us, O Lord.**
From all sin,	**deliver us, O Lord.**
From your just anger,	**deliver us, O Lord.**
From a sudden and unprovided death,	**deliver us, O Lord.**
From the snares of the devil,	**deliver us, O Lord.**
From anger, hatred, and feelings of revenge.	**deliver us, O Lord.**
From everlasting death,	**deliver us, O Lord.**
Through the mystery of your holy Incarnation,	**deliver us, O Lord.**
Through your coming,	**deliver us, O Lord.**
Through your nativity,	**deliver us, O Lord.**
Through your baptism and holy fasting,	**deliver us, O Lord.**
Through your cross and passion,	**deliver us, O Lord.**
Through your death and burial,	**deliver us, O Lord.**

Through your holy resurrection,	**deliver us, O Lord.**
Through your admirable ascension,	**deliver us, O Lord.**
Through the coming of the Holy Spirit, the comforter,	**deliver us, O Lord.**
In the day of judgment,	**deliver us, O Lord.**
We sinners,	**we beseech you, hear us.**
That you would spare us,	**we beseech you, hear us.**
That you would pardon us,	**we beseech you, hear us.**
That you would bring us to true penance,	**we beseech you, hear us.**
That you would govern and preserve your holy Church,	**we beseech you, hear us.**
That you would preserve our Pope and all ministers,	**we beseech you, hear us.**
That you would give peace and true concord, to Christian kings and queens,	**we beseech you, hear us.**
That you would grant peace and unity to all Christian people,	**we beseech you, hear us.**
That you would bring back to the unity of the Church all those who have strayed away, and lead to the light of the gospel all unbelievers,	**we beseech you, hear us.**
That you would confirm and preserve us in your holy service,	**we beseech you, hear us.**
That you would lift up our minds to desire heaven,	**we beseech you, hear us.**
That you would render eternal blessing to all our benefactors,	**we beseech you, hear us.**

That you would give and preserve the fruits of the earth,	**we beseech you, hear us.**
That you would grant eternal rest to all the faithful departed,	**we beseech you, hear us.**
That you would graciously hear us,	**we beseech you, hear us.**
Son of God,	**we beseech you, hear us.**
Lamb of God, who takes away the sins of the world,	**spare us, O Lord.**
Lamb of God, who takes away the sins of the world,	**have mercy on us.**

Christ, hear us,
Christ, graciously hear us.
Lord, have mercy on us.
Christ, have mercy on us.
Lord, have mercy on us.

Our Father . . .

Let us pray.
O God, whose nature it is to have mercy and to spare, receive our petitions that we and all your servants, may through your compassion and goodness be mercifully absolved from all our sins and attain to eternal salvation through Christ, Our Lord. **Amen.**

Holy Souls

Death is not the ultimate victor for the Christian. The resurrection of Jesus Christ means that death is swallowed up in victory *1 Corinthians 15:55. This is the root cause and source of our joyful hope. We pray in the risen Lord for repose for the souls of those who have gone before us. Together one day we shall be with the Lord in heaven where* there will be no more death, and no more mourning or sadness. *Revelation 21:4.*

Prayers for the dead

For the departed
Out of the depths I cry to you, O Lord,
Lord, hear my voice!
O let your ears be attentive
to the voice of my pleading.

If you, O Lord, should mark our guilt,
Lord, who would survive?
But with you is found forgiveness:
for this we revere you.

My soul is waiting for the Lord,
I count on his word.
My soul is longing for the Lord
more than watchman for daybreak.
(Let the watchman count on daybreak
and Israel on the Lord.)

Because with the Lord there is mercy
and fullness of redemption,

Israel indeed he will redeem
from all its iniquity.

Psalm 129

O Lord hear my prayer.
And let my cry come to you.

Let us pray
O God, the creator and redeemer of all the faithful
grant to the souls of your servants the remission of all
their sins, that through our pious supplications they
may obtain that pardon which they have always
desired; who lives and reigns for ever and ever. **Amen.**

Jesu, by that shuddering dread which fell on thee;
Jesu, by that cold dismay which sicken'd thee;
Jesu, by that pang of heart which thrill'd in thee;
Jesu, by that mount of sins which crippled thee;
Jesu, by that sense of guilt which stifled thee;
Jesu, by that innocence which girdled thee;
Jesu, by that sanctity which reigned in thee;
Jesu, by that Godhead which was one with thee;
Jesu, spare these souls which are so dear to thee;
Who in prison, calm and patient, wait for thee;
Hasten, Lord, their hour, and bid them come to thee.
To that glorious home, where they shall ever gaze on
thee.

John Henry Newman

For deceased parents
O God, who has commanded us to honour our father
and mother; in your mercy have pity on the souls of
my father and mother, and forgive them their sins; and
bring me to see them in the joy of eternal brightness.
Through Christ our Lord. Amen.

For our loved ones

We seem to give them back to thee, O God, who gavest them to us. Yet as thou didst not lose them in giving, so do we not lose them by their return. Not as the world giveth, givest thou, O lover of souls. What thou givest, thou takest not away, for what is thine is ours also if we are thine. And life is eternal and love is immortal, and death is only an horizon, and an horizon is nothing save the limit of our sight. Lift us up, strong Son of God, that we may see further; cleanse our eyes that we may see more clearly: draw us closer to thyself that we may know ourselves to be nearer to our loved ones who are with thee. And while thou dost prepare a place for us, prepare us also for that happy place, that where thou art we may be also for evermore. Amen.

Bede Jarrett

When a baby has died

Heavenly Father, your ways are hidden from our eyes, comfort, we pray you, the parents who grieve at the loss of their baby. Grant them grace to face the future with courage and gallantry. May they understand in faith that your love, as a Father, will not cause them a needless tear and that they will meet again in a fuller life those whose earthly body they prepared on earth.

Michael Buckley

For the departed

Receive, Lord, in tranquillity and peace, the souls of your servants who have departed out of this present life to be with you. Give them the life that knows no age, the good things that do not pass away; through Jesus Christ our Lord.

Saint Ignatius Loyola

Bona Mors
(devotions for a happy death)

Lord, have mercy,	**Lord, have mercy.**
Christ, have mercy,	**Christ, have mercy.**
Lord, have mercy,	**Lord, have mercy.**
Holy Mary,	**pray for us.**
All you holy angels and archangels,	**pray for us.**
All the choirs of the saints,	**pray for us.**
Saint John the baptist,	**pray for us.**
Saint Joseph,	**pray for us.**
All you holy patriarchs and prophets,	**pray for us.**
Saint Peter,	**pray for us.**
Saint Paul,	**pray for us.**
Saint Andrew,	**pray for us.**
Saint John,	**pray for us.**
All you holy apostles and evangelists,	**pray for us.**
All you holy doctors of our Lord,	**pray for us.**
All you holy innocents,	**pray for us.**
Saint Stephen,	**pray for us.**
Saint Lawrence,	**pray for us.**
All you holy martyrs,	**pray for us.**
Saint Sylvester,	**pray for us.**
Saint Gregory,	**pray for us.**
Saint Augustine,	**pray for us.**
All you holy bishops and confessors,	**pray for us.**
Saint Benedict,	**pray for us.**
Saint Francis,	**pray for us.**
Saint Camillus,	**pray for us.**
Saint John of God,	**pray for us.**
All you holy monks and hermits,	**pray for us.**

Saint Mary Magdalen,	**pray for us.**
Saint Lucy,	**pray for us.**
All you holy virgins and widows,	**pray for us.**
All you saints of God,	**intercede for us.**
Be merciful,	**spare us, O Lord.**
Be merciful,	**hear us, O Lord.**
Be merciful,	**deliver us, O Lord.**
From the peril of death,	**deliver us, O Lord.**
From all evil,	**deliver us, O Lord.**
From the power of the devil,	**deliver us, O Lord.**
Through your nativity,	**deliver us, O Lord.**
Through your cross and passion,	**deliver us, O Lord.**
Through your death and burial,	**deliver us, O Lord.**
Through your glorious resurrection,	**deliver us, O Lord.**
Through your wonderful ascension,	**deliver us, O Lord.**
Through the grace of the Holy Spirit, the comforter,	**deliver us, O Lord.**

Lord, have mercy on us.
Christ, have mercy on us.
Lord, have mercy on us.

We beseech your mercy O Lord, to strengthen your servants with your grace at the hour of death, that the enemy may not prevail over us, but that we may deserve to pass with your angels into everlasting life.

Almighty and most gracious God, who brought forth for your thirsting people a stream of living water from the rock, draw tears of true repentance from our stony hearts, that we may be sorry for our sins, gain forgiveness of them from your mercy and so attain to everlasting life.

Lord Jesus Christ, Redeemer of the world, behold us prostrate at your feet. With our whole heart we are sorry for our sins of thought, word and deed; and because we love you and will ever love you above all created things, we are resolved with the help of your grace, never more to offend you.

O Jesus, who during your prayer to the Father in the garden was filled with so much sorrow and anguish that your sweat became as drops of blood; have mercy on us.

Have mercy on us, O Lord; have mercy on us.

O Jesus, betrayed by the kiss of a traitor into the hands of the wicked, seized and bound like a thief, and forsaken by your disciples; have mercy on us.

Have mercy on us, O Lord; have mercy on us.

O Jesus, sentenced to death, led like a malefactor before Pilate, scorned and derided by Herod; have mercy on us.

Have mercy on us, O Lord; have mercy on us.

O Jesus, stripped of your garments, and cruelly scourged at the pillar; have mercy on us.

Have mercy on us, O Lord; have mercy on us.

O Jesus, crowned with thorns, buffeted, struck with a reed, blindfolded, clothed with a purple garment, and overwhelmed with reproaches; have mercy on us.

Have mercy on us, O Lord; have mercy on us.

O Jesus, loaded with a cross, and led to the place of execution as a lamb to the slaughter; have mercy on us.

Have mercy on us, O Lord; have mercy on us.

O Jesus, numbered among thieves, blasphemed and derided, offered gall and vinegar to drink, and crucified in dreadful torment from the sixth to the ninth hour; have mercy on us.

Have mercy on us, O Lord; have mercy on us.

O Jesus, who expired on the cross, was pierced with a lance in the presence of your holy Mother, and from whose side poured forth blood and water; have mercy on us.

Have mercy on us, O Lord; have mercy on us.

O Jesus, taken down from the cross, and bathed in the tears of your sorrowing virgin Mother; have mercy on us.

Have mercy on us, O Lord; have mercy on us.

O Jesus, covered with bruises, marked with the five wounds, embalmed with spices, and laid in the sepulchre; have mercy on us.

Have mercy on us, O Lord; have mercy on us.

O Jesus, who rose from the dead by the power of the Father and so became the source of our own resurrection; have mercy on us.

Have mercy on us, O Lord; have mercy on us.

He has truly borne our sorrows.

And he has carried our griefs.

Let us pray.
O God, whose only Son, Jesus Christ, underwent death so that in his own flesh he might conquer it, help us by meditating on his passion, death and resurrection to put aside our unholy fear of death and see it as the gateway through which we must pass in our journey to eternal life. **Amen.**

Acknowledgements

The compiler and publisher wish to express their gratitude to the following for permission to reproduce or adapt material of which they are the authors, publishers, or copyright holders. An asterisk indicates that the prayer has been adapted.

Excerpts from the English translation of *The Roman Missal* © 1973, International Committee on English in the Liturgy, Inc. All rights reserved.

Excerpts from *The Jerusalem Bible*, copyright © 1966 by Darton, Longman & Todd, Ltd. and Doubleday & Company, Inc. Reprinted by permission of the publisher.

Catholic Truth Society for one prayer from the *Simple Prayer Book*.

Fontana Paperbacks for three prayers by William Barclay from *The Plain Man's Book of Prayers*.

Lutterworth Press for three prayers by George Appleton.

Augsburg Publishing House for two prayers reprinted by permission from *Diary of Daily Prayer* by J. Barrie Shepherd, copyright Augsburg Publishing House.

Mayhew McCrimmon Ltd. publishers of *The One Who Listens* for the prayers by Michael Hollings and Etta Gullick. Used with permission. All rights reserved.

Oxford University Press for three prayers by John Baillie from *A Diary of Private Prayer* (OUP 1936) and one by Eric Milner-White from *Daily Prayer*, edited by